THE POSITIVE KINGDOM

Colin Urquhart

HODDER AND STOUGHTON
LONDON AUCKLAND SYDNEY TORONTO

British Library Cataloguing in Publication Data

Urquhart, Colin
   The positive kingdom.—(Hodder Christian
paperbacks)
   1. Christian life
   I. Title
   248.4   BV4501.2

   ISBN 0 340 36478 5

Hodder and Stoughton Editorial Office: 47 Bedford Square, London WC1B 3DP

For all those who feel they have little or no hope; that they may come to know the power of the Positive Kingdom in their lives.

Acknowledgements

My thanks to all those who have helped with the preparation of this book – those with whom I share in the life of the Positive Kingdom. Principally that means my wife, Caroline, who is such an encouragement to me in my ministry; and my children Claire, Clive and Andrea, who are greatly used by the Lord to remind me that Kingdom living has to be an earthly business! My thanks to all the members of my household and of the Bethany Fellowship, especially to Annette, for all her typing, and to Barbara.

The Scripture quotations are from the New International Version, except where stated.

Contents

Chapter 1

OUR POSITIVE GOD

Jesus came to give you a Kingdom! A Kingdom with resources far beyond those of any earthly kingdom. An eternal Kingdom. If you receive the gift of this Kingdom now, you can reign with Him for all eternity.

Great claims! But then Jesus makes staggering promises to those who believe in Him. It is God's intention for you to possess the Kingdom of heaven now. Yet many Christians have gained the impression, or have even been taught, that this Kingdom can be entered only beyond death, and that there is always an element of uncertainty as to whether they will actually be accepted by God.

Our Heavenly Father intends us to know we have received the Kingdom as a gift from Him, not because we deserve such generosity, or are able to make ourselves worthy of such a gift, but because He is the God of grace; He gives His everything although we deserve nothing.

The phrases 'Kingdom of heaven' and 'Kingdom of God' are used interchangeably in the New Testament. The Kingdom of God is the Kingdom of heaven; the Kingdom of heaven is the Kingdom of God.

He wants you to know you have received His gift and He wants to teach you how to live in the power of His Kingdom; to be a Kingdom child living His Kingdom life, filled with His Kingdom power, using His Kingdom authority, drawing constantly on His Kingdom resources by exercising Kingdom faith.

How can these things be a practical reality for you? First, realise that the Kingdom reflects the nature of the King.

There is a principle that runs through several areas of our experience. The life of a nation reflects the nature of the government of that nation. It may have a democratically elected government or be a totalitarian state. In either case the policies and decisions of government will be worked out in the life of the nation.

The same principle applies in business. The policy decisions of management are worked out on the shop-floor and in the marketing of the product. In a school, the nature of the headship will determine the whole ethos of the institution, its discipline, priorities and objectives. In the home the leadership of the parents, and particularly the father, will be reflected in the whole family. The children are the product of the kind of headship that is exercised over them.

Any congregation or fellowship reflects the nature of the spiritual and pastoral leadership given by those in authority. You may find individual believers blessed or anointed by God beyond anything experienced by their leaders. Nevertheless, the congregation as a whole cannot grow beyond the example given by those in leadership; the people can only go where they are led.

The principle, then, is clear. Those in authority have a profound effect on those over whom they have authority.

This is supremely true of God's Kingdom: *the Kingdom of heaven reflects the nature of the King of heaven*. So if we want to know what kind of a Kingdom God offers us, we need to see what kind of a God He is.

THE KING

Everything about God is positive. There are no negatives in Him.

God is holy. He is whole, complete and perfect in Himself. He is above and beyond all He has made. Something of His beauty and majesty can be seen in His creation and yet He is far greater than creation, remembering that this planet is only a minute part of all He has made.

God is righteous. He is right in all He does. It is His nature to be right and He cannot deny Himself. He is the absolute standard by which everything and everyone is judged. Whatever He does is right by definition. Whatever opposes Him or His ways is unrighteous.

God is just. Again it is by His standards that true justice is to be assessed. He has never acted unjustly towards anyone. It is in His justice that He declares that sinners are worthy of death, eternal condemnation and separation from Him – a godless eternity. That is not what He wants for His people, but it is what they deserve, because the unholy and the unrighteous cannot be made one with the Holy and Righteous, unless they are first cleansed of their ungodliness. Equally, it is in justice that He declares sinners 'not guilty' when they ask for His forgiveness. Jesus carried their guilt to the cross, and paid the price for their sins with His own death.

God is love. In His love He sends His Son to live a godly life among men, and to offer His sinless life as a sacrifice on behalf of all sinners. God's love does not change with emotion like human love; it is steadfast, sure and dependable. It is a love that must be given, shared and communicated to those He loves. It is a love that knows no limits.

God is gracious. If He dealt with people as they deserved, He would wipe them off the face of the earth. Instead He offers them His Kingdom. In His grace He is willing to give His riches to those who deserve nothing.

God is almighty. He has demonstrated His almightiness in creation. Nothing is impossible for Him. Through Jesus, He has shown He has the power over sin, sickness and even death. He is the God who raises up nations and has the power to cause them to fall. He is working His purpose out and there is nothing able to prevent the fulfilment of His plans.

God is life. He alone could give life to man at a natural level.

He alone can impart His own supernatural life, the gift of eternal life. He sent His Son that men might receive that life in all its fullness.

God is joy. When the Father speaks of His own Son, He declares: 'God, your God, has set you above your companions by anointing you with the oil of joy.' (Heb. 1: 9) He causes heaven to rejoice over all sinners who repent. The words Jesus gives His disciples makes their joy full and complete, and God's purpose for us is to rejoice in Him always.

God is peace. Jesus gave His peace to His disciples before His crucifixion, and greeted them with His peace when He appeared to them in His risen body. His peace is a positive gift such as the world is unable to give, a peace that is beyond understanding or description. The peace of God is not simply the absence of war, noise or anxiety. It comes from having a sense of well-being with God, even in the midst of turmoil and difficulties.

God is the provider. Again and again He assures His people of His willingness to meet their every need, if they remain faithful and obedient to Him. Jesus gives a series of startling prayer promises, indicating it is His Father's purpose to give His people anything they ask in His name. In His love He *wants* to give to His children and provide for them.

God is the healer. Throughout His earthly ministry Jesus demonstrated His Father's desire to heal. He had not come to do His own thing, but to perform the will of His Father who sent Him. He said He could do nothing Himself; He did only what He saw His Father doing. Clearly then it is God's desire to bring healing, in the fullest sense of that word, into the lives of His people.

God is truth. There is nothing false about God. The words He speaks both through the prophets in the Old Testament and His Son in the New, prove to be true because they have their source in the one who will not deceive. Jesus proclaims that He is the truth and His Spirit, given to those who believe in Him, will guide them into all truth.

God is faithful. He is always reliable and dependable, and so are His words. He abides by the promises He gives. Even when His children prove unfaithful to Him, He remains faithful to them.

This is only a partial list of God's attributes, but enough to show that everything about Him is positive. He is holy, righteous, just, loving, gracious, almighty, life-giving, joyful, peace, the Provider, the Healer, the truth, the faithful one.

Above all *God is our Father.* He reveals Himself to His people as having personality, and demonstrates that He wants them to have a personal relationship with Him. He sends His Son to die on the cross to make such a relationship possible.

We are not to judge the fatherhood of God by our experience of human fathers. Even the best human father would only be a poor reflection of God as Father. All human fatherhood is to be seen in relationship to Him, not the other way round. He is the perfect Father and the Scriptures reveal Him as the holy Father, the righteous Father and the loving Father who is not afraid to discipline His children.

God is our Saviour. Without His atoning work on the cross it would not be possible for sinful men to be reconciled with the sinless God. Because He is the Saviour He sends His Son to perform that work of salvation whereby we may be justified, or made acceptable to God, and able to receive the gift of His Kingdom.

Everything He is and everything He does is positive. Even the wrath of God is positive: God dealing positively with those who positively need to be dealt with! He is the Judge whose judgments are always just.

Because it reflects the nature of the King, the Kingdom is holy, righteous and just; a Kingdom of love and power. Those who belong to it experience not only these qualities of God's life, but also His grace, joy and peace. They can receive His promises and healing and know their lives are led by the God who is both truthful and faithful. He is their Father, who by

His own initiative has given them salvation and the gift of eternal life.

Everything about the King is positive; therefore everything about His Kingdom is positive.

Chapter 2

THE NEGATIVE WORLD

It is immediately obvious that we live in a world in which we encounter many negatives. We can see why Jesus said: 'My kingdom is not of this world.' (John 18: 36) He came from the Father to bring His positive Kingdom into this negative world. This at once raises the question which has plagued mankind: 'Why does the negative exist if God is positive and His Kingdom positive?'

We must understand that there are two spiritual kingdoms – not one. There is the Kingdom of God or the Kingdom of heaven, which is the Kingdom of light. There is also the dominion of Satan, the kingdom of darkness, where everything is negative.

Just as the Kingdom of God reflects the nature of the one who rules over it, so does the dominion of darkness.

Satan was once the archangel Lucifer enjoying the glory of God's heavenly Kingdom. He became discontent leading others to worship God and decided it was time he was worshipped himself. He wanted to be as God instead of honouring Him.

His rebellion against the Lord led to his immediate dismissal from heaven, along with the angels who followed him. Jesus said: 'I saw Satan fall like lightning from heaven.' (Luke 10: 18) He no longer has access to heaven; but ever since his fall has done all he can to incite others to rebel against God.

Jesus describes him as the thief who comes only to steal, kill and destroy. He is a liar from the beginning, the father of all lies, the deceiver. He is the tempter who even tried to tempt Jesus in the wilderness. He is God's enemy, and ours too! What a contrast to the Positive God!

Everything about Satan is negative and he wants to create the negative in people's lives.

He was once holy and righteous, but now constantly tempts people to be unholy and unrighteous. He loves to cause injustice, hatred, sickness and poverty. His tactics vary. He encourages some to believe they are in his power; he persuades others not to believe in him at all. Supremely, he wants to encourage people to worship him by practising black magic and witchcraft.

When we are born into this world we belong to the kingdom of this world. Because of our fallen nature, we belong to the kingdom of darkness, not the Kingdom of light. Like Satan, we instinctively want our own way. Through our sin and disobedience we rebel against God. We are full of unbelief and are often the victims of fear and sickness. Many are soon caught, even at an early age, in a web of lies, intrigue and deception.

The majority of people do not know God in a loving, personal relationship, and many even deny His existence. Relatively few truly desire His will for their lives.

It is Satan's ultimate deception to encourage people to believe that everyone will go to heaven in the end, regardless of their religious beliefs or practices. If they doubt the reality of his existence, they will question the existence of hell or the possibility of a Godless eternity.

The evidence of the negative in the world around us is too obvious to need much comment. But does God intend people to live their lives dominated by negative spiritual forces and experiences?

GOD'S ANSWER

The gospel of Jesus Christ is good news. It is obvious from His teaching that God desires to free people from the negative. He came and 'rescued us from the dominion of darkness and brought us into the kingdom of the Son he loves'. (Col. 1: 13)

For God to free His people from rebellion, sin and disobedience, a rescue act was needed. He wanted to free them from fear and want, from sickness and poverty. He wanted to give them life – His life in all its fullness, positive life. Instead of deception He wanted to see the hearts and lives of His people full of truth and love. He wanted a people who knew His love, experienced His joy, enjoyed His peace and depended on His faithfulness.

God sent Jesus to save His people: save them from the dominion of darkness; save them from sin, fear and unbelief; save them from condemnation to a Godless eternity, the judgment hanging over all who do not belong to the Kingdom of heaven. To save them, then, from hell and restore to them the gift of eternal life.

Anyone is lost until he sees the need of a Saviour, someone to rescue him from himself and to give him a Kingdom, not only as a future hope, but as a present reality.

The opening words of Jesus's ministry were a brief command and mighty promise from God: 'Repent, for the kingdom of heaven is near.' (Matt. 4: 17)

With the coming of the Son of God from heaven the Kingdom of heaven was now brought within the reach of men; it was 'at hand'. Until then it could only have been a future hope, a possibility. Now it became actual in the lives of those who repented, who turned their lives over to Jesus, recognising His sovereign reign and rule in their lives.

That act of repentance had to be coupled with faith in Him: 'The kingdom of God is near. Repent and believe the good news!' (Mark 1: 15) Men's lives need no longer be dominated by the negative. Satan need no longer be their master. The prince of this world may have dominated their lives in the past, but having submitted their lives to the King of heaven they can know and experience the glorious liberty of the sons of God. The prince of this world stands condemned. He can no longer usurp the rightful place of God in the life of anyone who submits to Jesus, the King of heaven and earth.

Later Jesus was to unfold a simple but astonishing truth to the disciples: 'Do not be afraid, little flock, for your Father has been pleased to give you the kingdom.' (Luke 12: 32)

That is the truth, amazing as it may seem. The Father sent His Son so that all who received Him and believed in Him would be given the Kingdom of God. Jesus came so believers could receive the Kingdom now and thereby receive all that is positive. He made it possible for their negative lives to be transformed into positive ones.

There was no way that they, or anybody else, could deserve to receive such a gift from God, no way in which they could earn entrance into His Kingdom. It is only by the grace and mercy of the God of love that a person can be given such an inheritance.

If we try to see the situation from God's perspective we shall gain some insight into His purpose. He had created man in His own image, to be like Him. The human race was to reflect His nature, character and personality. In the story of Adam and Eve we see what God wanted: men and women living in close union and fellowship with Him and with one another; sinless, innocent, with provision made for all their needs.

Everything in their lives was positive. But along comes Satan with his negative temptation. First Eve, and then Adam, are tempted to disobey God, to deny the word He had spoken to them. When they lose their innocence by yielding to temptation, they want to hide from God and from one another. The beauty of their fellowship is shattered. Now they are sinners, have to work to survive and are excluded from the garden paradise.

Sin has entered their lives. The negative has infected what before was completely positive. Now the image of God in them is marred.

None of this caught the Lord by surprise. He knew it would happen, would even be inevitable, if He was to create a creature with free-will, the freedom to love or hate, obey or disobey. Now He sees His people pursuing their own ways instead of His, intent on fulfilling their own lusts and desires, infected through and through with the rebellion of Satan. Their lives become confused by the introduction of so many negative elements. Now they curse and blaspheme; they are full of selfishness and pride. They create their own false gods to worship and their hatred leads them to destroy one another.

GOD'S OWN PEOPLE

Among all this confusion God is determined to have a people for Himself, a holy people who will reflect His own holiness, who will love Him and worship only Him, who will be loyal and obedient to Him, fulfilling the commandments He gives them. He chooses the Israelites to be such a people. He reveals His almightiness and love by delivering them from the oppression of their Egyptian overlords. Through Moses He gives them the commandments they are to obey and the promises He will fulfil whenever they prove obedient.

Again and again, He sees His people turning away from Him whenever they prosper, and seeking Him only when their plight is desperate. He has those who remain faithful, the prophets who address the mass of the people, calling them to repentance and warning them of the consequences if they fail to do so. Time and again His spokesmen are ignored and the people persist in their rebellion and disobedience.

Before the creation of the world, God had determined what He would do. There was no alternative but to become man Himself. He would take human flesh as Jesus Christ, the Son of God. The Word that had been spoken for centuries from heaven would now dwell among men, so that all could hear His voice clearly.

God the Father sends His Son to rescue His people from all the effects of the negative, from sin, fear, unbelief and sickness. He sees that many refuse to hear Him, especially the religious ones – those intent on serving God by obeying their traditions, those with the outward form of religion but lacking the inner reality of a living relationship with God. He sees their opposition, fear and determination to do away with His Son.

On the other hand, God sees many recognising their need of a saviour and turning to Him for forgiveness, deliverance and healing. He watches over His Son as He proclaims the good news that He has been sent by His Father with the gift of God's Kingdom. He sees some believing, while others use their free-will to pursue their own ways.

The Father sees His Son gather around Him a group of disciples, who can be taught the principles of the Kingdom and how to live as those who receive divine authority from heaven. His Son performs the works of the Kingdom among the people, healing the sick, raising the dead, cleansing lepers, casting out demons and performing many miraculous signs.

However, Jesus has to do more than speak about the Kingdom and demonstrate its imminence with His presence in the world; He has to do what is necessary to make it possible for sinners to be received into the Kingdom. His mission would have been a failure if He had demonstrated an unattainable Kingdom to the people. They had to understand that God was prepared to forgive them for all the ways in which they had been negative, under the dominance of the prince of this world, and that He was willing to pour His own positive life into them. They needed a Saviour!

Chapter 3

THE CROSS

The cross was a necessity to enable sinners to enter and possess the Kingdom of God. There Jesus offered to the Father His holy life on behalf of all those tainted by unholiness, His righteous life for all who had lived in unrighteousness or self-righteousness, believing they could make themselves acceptable to God. It was on the cross that Jesus gave His perfect life for the imperfect, His sinless life for sinners. He gave to the Father the one, complete sacrifice that was necessary to satisfy the just demands of the Holy, Righteous and Loving Judge. The Sinless One had to die for sinners. His life-blood had to be poured out in sacrifice that they might be able to receive God's life.

The Father led His own Son to that cross because of His love for the world. He watches over the agony of decision in the Garden of Gethsemane, over the harsh and rude repudiation of His divinity in His rejection, beatings and mock crowning. He sees the desolation of the cross when His Son hangs in pain, so totally identified with the depravity of sinful humanity that He cries out, 'My God, my God, why have you forsaken me?' (Mark 15: 34)

When Jesus went to the cross, He took all the negatives that men experience so that they may be delivered from them. He took all their sins; He carried their sicknesses, spiritual, emotional and physical. He took their conflicts and all that make them lose peace with God, with one another and with themselves. He suffered rejection from the religious authorities, from the state, from the people and even His own disciples, so that we might be freed from every experience of rejection.

'Surely he took up our infirmities and carried our sorrows, yet we considered him stricken by God, smitten by him, and afflicted. But he was pierced for our transgressions, he was crushed for our iniquities; the punishment that brought us peace was upon him, and by his wounds we are healed.' (Isa. 53: 4–5) He even suffered the punishment that we deserve so that we do not have to suffer it.

What a God of love, mercy and grace! He deals with all the negatives to make us able to receive His positive life.

He raises His Son, demonstrating that His Kingdom is eternal and victorious over death. During the forty days of His resurrection appearances to His disciples, He continues to teach them about the Kingdom. Then the Father receives Him back into the glory of that Kingdom so that, as the sacrificial Lamb slain for His people, He could reign with Him for all eternity. 'Worthy is the Lamb, who was slain, to receive power and wealth and wisdom and strength and honour and glory and praise!' (Rev. 5: 12)

This is victory indeed. Now to every man there is a sacrifice available, able to cleanse him from his sins and make him acceptable to God. Now there can be freedom from the negative for all who come to the cross and put their faith in Jesus and what He has accomplished for them. Now the way is cleared for people to receive the gift of the positive Kingdom that Jesus makes available.

NEW BIRTH

It is inconceivable to some that God should simply *give* them an eternal Kingdom. If God is so great, so much higher and more holy than men, then surely they should work hard with every part of their being to make themselves acceptable to Him? Surely they have to earn the right to participate in God's Kingdom? Does not Jesus teach that a man will be judged by the works he has done?

Such attitudes are the result of pride, not of humility. What can anyone do to atone for his own sins? How can a sinner make himself acceptable in the sight of the holy God, no matter how many good deeds he claims?

Certainly church membership does not make a man acceptable to God; neither can his religious opinions, attitudes or works justify him. It is only the work of Jesus Himself, the Saviour, that can undo his sinfulness and make the repentant sinner a saint – someone whose life is made holy in God's sight, someone set apart for His glory, someone who becomes a child of God's Kingdom.

It was to Nicodemus, a Pharisee, a man brought up in strict religious traditions, to whom Jesus said: 'I tell you the truth, unless a man is born again, he cannot see the kingdom of God.' (John 3: 3)

He uses the phrase 'I tell you the truth' when He knows that what He is about to say will be met with unbelief; it will be hard to hear and receive such revelation. To be part of this Kingdom a man *must* be born again. There can be no compromise on that statement of truth. To Jesus it is a fact and the matter is not open to debate.

The only people (whether they go to church or not) who do not like talk of being born again are those who have never experienced a second birth. It is only the unconverted man who feels resentful when challenged as to whether he has been converted or born again!

Jesus explains: 'Flesh gives birth to flesh, but the Spirit gives birth to spirit.' (John 3: 6) When each of us is born into the world, we are born in flesh. Our birth is the result of a physical relationship between a man and woman. We are born with a fallen sinful nature, will inevitably sin, displease God and need a Saviour.

When we are cleansed from our sins through that perfect, sinless sacrifice of Jesus on the cross then, and only then, can we be 'born from above' and experience a personal relationship with God whereby we know Him intimately as

'Father'.

This second birth is the result of the activity of God's own Holy Spirit bringing to life the human spirit of the repentant sinner. He is then born of the Spirit. Jesus emphasises the point: 'I tell you the truth, unless a man is born of water and the Spirit, he cannot enter the kingdom of God.' (John 3: 5)

Baptism in water signifies that a man has come to personal repentance, acknowledging Jesus as his Saviour, and a personal faith in Him, submitting to Him as the Lord of his life. Baptism is not a magical formula that brings a person into the Kingdom of God apart from repentance and faith. Rather, it signifies that the sinner has taken off his old life of opposition to the purposes of God, and has put on the new life of Jesus, made possible only through His redeeming love, mercy and grace. He recognises that Jesus purchased him for heaven; He paid the price that no other could ever pay. The cost was the shedding of His own blood.

Once the sinner identifies with the work of Jesus on the cross by repentance and faith, then he is set free from his past with all its rebellion, fear, doubt and sin. He is born again, is given a new beginning to his life; he has become a new creation. 'The old has gone, the new has come!' (2 Cor. 5: 17)

There can be no avoiding this fundamental truth of the gospel of Jesus Christ: a man *must* be born again to be part of God's Kingdom. Once he has experienced that new birth, the glorious possibilities of what it means to be part of that Kingdom begin to unfold before him.

It is possible to attend church services for years, even as ministers and leaders, yet without a saving experience of new birth, or a heart revelation of being God's Kingdom children. When churchmen are born again, their lives, ministries and preaching are transformed. Nicodemus and Saul of Tarsus were very religious men, devoted to serving God and pleasing Him; yet Jesus had to teach both their need of new birth if they were to be men of the Kingdom. And what a glorious transformation came about in the life of the one who had persecuted the early Christians, when he experienced new birth: he became the apostle to the Gentiles.

I constantly meet faithful church members, who have only recently experienced new birth in Jesus and the power of the Holy Spirit in their lives. I am frequently asked such questions as: 'Why did nobody tell us such things were possible before? Why did we have to wait all these years?' Why indeed!

INCLUSIVE OR EXCLUSIVE?

Some object that this teaching is exclusive; it excludes the vast majority from entering God's Kingdom. They want an inclusive gospel, a universal one through which all men will enter God's Kingdom. They point out that it was for His love of the whole world that God sent His Son, and He died on the cross for all mankind. 'Everyone will be all right in the end' is a popular notion, but totally contradicting New Testament teaching.

The truth is that the gospel is both inclusive and exclusive. It is true that Christ came to die for all sinners, and that through His sacrifice salvation becomes a possibility for all men. However it is also true that only those who come to personal repentance and faith receive the benefit of His cross. It is only they who experience new life, because they have been cleansed from their sins and made acceptable to God. It is only they who are able to receive the gift of His Kingdom.

Jesus took all men to the cross, but it is only those who repent and believe in Him who are raised to new life. The cross is inclusive, making salvation possible for all men; the Kingdom is exclusive, and is for those whose lives are submitted to the sovereignty of the heavenly King, by their personal repentance and faith.

AS LITTLE CHILDREN

Jesus said: 'Therefore I tell you that the kingdom of God will be taken away from you and given to a people who will produce its fruit.' (Matt. 21: 43) As in the time of Jesus, so today. He warns that there will be some who imagine they will be accepted into the Kingdom, but who have never produced the fruit seen in those who are already children of the Kingdom.

God is not the harsh judge who desires to exclude people. Quite the opposite: He teaches His disciples to gather people into the Kingdom and He dies to make it possible for all who repent and believe to receive that rich inheritance.

The plain fact is that many refuse to repent; some see no reason why they should, perhaps because they have never heard the gospel truly proclaimed.

'Let the little children come to me, and do not hinder them, for the kingdom of heaven belongs to such as these.' (Matt. 19: 14) This is not a sentimental picture of Jesus blessing children, to be framed and hung on walls at Sunday Schools, but a profound statement of truth about the nature of the Kingdom of God.

Jesus does not say the Kingdom belongs to little children but to 'such as these' – those who come humbly and trustingly to Him; those who don't argue against, or question, His authority. Little children or grown adults can enter the Kingdom and know Jesus as their Lord; but only as they submit their lives to the authority of the King.

This is the beginning of a continual process of submission. At several stages of their development children will need to submit their lives afresh to Jesus. *They are to grow up in Him, not away from Him.*

TRUE RIGHTEOUSNESS

So He makes it clear that 'unless your righteousness surpasses that of the Pharisees and the teachers of the law, you will certainly not enter the kingdom of heaven.' (Matt. 5: 20) For all their religious fervour they were not part of the Kingdom; nor would they ever be unless they were born again.

Neither an appearance of godliness nor an external moral fervour would satisfy Jesus. He saw straight to men's hearts where good or bad fruit originate. The righteousness that concerned Him began with the heart, a man being in right relationship and right standing with God.

Later Jesus was to describe the teachers of the law and the Pharisees as hypocrites. They were concerned about petty details but neglected such essentials as justice, mercy and faithfulness. They were concerned about outward appearances, but inwardly were full of greed and self-indulgence, of dead men's bones and everything unclean; they were full of hypocrisy and wickedness. Their hearts were negative.

The righteousness Jesus gives is of a totally different order. Through the shedding of His own blood, those who believe in Him have all their sin and guilt washed away and are given new hearts. Christians are put right with God through the blood of the cross, and enabled to live righteous lives through the power of the Holy Spirit, who is God coming to live in His people.

Such righteousness exceeds that of the scribes and Pharisees and is only possible through Jesus. They chose to hang on to their superficial self-righteousness (which is as filthy rags to God), instead of recognising their need of a change of heart. They felt threatened by Jesus's teaching and actions and wanted to destroy Him, rather than repent and submit to His authority.

There is no righteousness acceptable to God except that obtainable through Jesus Christ. Without His righteousness 'you will certainly not enter the kingdom of heaven'.

Chapter 4

RECEIVING THE KINGDOM

For three years Jesus taught about the positive Kingdom and performed the supernatural works that demonstrated the nature of this Kingdom. 'Jesus went throughout Galilee, teaching in their synagogues, preaching the good news of the kingdom, and healing every disease and sickness among the people.' (Matt. 4: 23) He refused to remain too long in one place, saying: 'I must preach the good news of the kingdom of God to the other towns also, because that is why I was sent.' (Luke 4: 43) He 'travelled about from one town and village to another, proclaiming the good news of the kingdom of God.' (Luke 8: 1)

GOOD NEWS

The revelation of the Kingdom is good news! It is good news that men can be delivered from the kingdom of darkness and brought into the Kingdom of light. It is good news that they can be released from any bondage to Satan and be brought into the freedom of God's reign. It is good news that God is a loving Father, who sacrifices His own Son on the cross to enable many sons to be born into His Kingdom. It is good news that He is a God of such infinite grace and mercy, that He is willing to forgive the sins of those who repent and promises His Kingdom life and power to those who believe.

Having received the revelation that God offers a Kingdom to those who believe in Him, how could anyone be so foolish as to refuse such a wonderful offer?

Paul says: 'The kingdom of God is not a matter of talk but of power.' (1 Cor. 4: 20) Jesus demonstrated this truth in His own ministry. Along with the spoken revelation of the Kingdom went the visible manifestations of the power of that Kingdom. He did not expect people to believe a gospel of words without giving evidence of the truth of what He said. From the very beginning His gospel was confirmed with signs following, which demonstrated the imminence of the Kingdom He came to make available. He welcomed the crowds and 'spoke to them about the kingdom of God, and healed those who needed healing.' (Luke 9: 11)

He did not want their concentration to be on the signs but on the revelation of the Kingdom. But wherever His words were met with faith, the positive power of God's Kingdom overcame the negative problems in people's lives. By that power Jesus healed the sick, raised the dead and delivered people from bondage to evil spirits.

When the gospel of the Kingdom takes effect in people's lives there are powerful consequences.

Everything Jesus said relates in one way or another to the Kingdom. At the beginning of the Sermon on the Mount He says: 'Blessed are the poor in spirit, for theirs is the kingdom of heaven.' (Matt. 5: 3) The poor in spirit are those who recognise their spiritual poverty without Jesus. They know their need of God and are prepared to turn to Him in repentance, putting their faith in His grace and mercy. Their salvation depends on God alone and the mighty love He has poured out for them.

Such people are blessed, which the Amplified Bible describes as 'happy, to be envied and spiritually prosperous (that is, with life-joy and satisfaction in God's favour and salvation, regardless of their outward conditions).' (Matt. 5: 3)

The poor in spirit recognise their nothingness before the Almighty and Holy God. And yet because the Son of God became poor, they are made rich! They already possess the Kingdom.

REPENTANCE

What does repentance involve? Literally, a change of mind, a turning to God.

Paul points out that: 'The god of this age has blinded the minds of unbelievers, so that they cannot see the light of the gospel of the glory of Christ, who is the image of God.' (2 Cor. 4: 4) When a man receives revelation, light begins to penetrate his spiritual darkness. He sees that he is a sinner needing God's salvation, and senses Jesus calling him to the cross that he may be cleansed and born again.

That does not necessarily mean he will respond to God's call. Because of his love of sin, or desire to live independently of God's authority, he may choose to remain in his sins, alienated and cut off from the Lord. He will not know peace until he has a change of mind and is prepared to submit to the Lordship of Jesus Christ.

Revelation that God wants to give him His Kingdom will encourage the sinner to 'turn around', to turn his life over to God. Until he repents, he will remain outside that Kingdom; when he does submit his life to God, he becomes a child of that Kingdom, with all its attendant privileges and responsibilities.

When he is prepared to respond to God's initiative in offering him His Kingdom, he will confess he is a sinner in need of a Saviour. He will ask Jesus to forgive everything in his life that has been opposed to God's purposes. There will be specific things about which he feels particularly convicted and guilty, which will need to be brought to Jesus for His forgiveness.

The sinner not only recognises he has done wrong; he *is* wrong and needs to be put right with God. He has lived in unbelief, or with only a token recognition of God in his life.

He needs to be cleansed, made acceptable to God, to be born again, and made a new person. And so he gives his life to Jesus. He wants Him to be his Lord and King, to rule and reign in every area of his life, for his body to become a temple of the Holy Spirit. He is prepared to submit his future to God, to be led and guided by Him; to use his time as He determines. He wants the Lord to reign in his relationships, family, work, the use of his money and property. He realises that God cannot be a side interest in his life; He has to become the centre around whom everything revolves.

This is indeed a change of mind. From leaving God out he now invites Him into everything.

Together with this repentance he expresses a personal faith in Jesus to forgive him, cleanse him, accept him and make him new; faith that He will love him and care for him, lead and guide him and bring him into His Kingdom for all eternity.

For some, the initial act of repentance is a very simple act of heart submission to God that leads to this thorough cleansing and change of life. For others, a yielding of themselves in detail is necessary. In either case, the newly-converted person needs to know that God will no longer hold against him the sins He has forgiven. He is completely free of the guilt and punishment that his sins deserved, for even his punishment was suffered by Jesus on his behalf.

The Spirit of God, now living in him, will enable him to follow obediently in the way that Jesus leads him, to live as a child of His Kingdom. He is highly valued by God and greatly privileged to have received every spiritual gift that God has in heavenly places.

GOD'S SUPERNATURAL LIFE

Some people attend church services for years without ever being challenged with their need to repent, or to express personal faith in Jesus and His Word. You cannot separate God from His Word. To have a relationship with Him, once you are born again, means that the Holy Spirit will want to lead you into the truth of God's Word.

Some pride themselves on their power of rational thinking, saying that God has given them the ability to reason for themselves. They think nothing of picking and choosing from the Scriptures the things that accord with their own thinking, denying what offends them as unreasonable.

As a result there are many congregations where there is a great fear of the supernatural. God is supernatural and the Kingdom He gives is supernatural. To remove the supernatural from the Bible leaves you only the cover! It is the revelation of the supernatural God working supernaturally in the lives of His people.

Jesus tells Nicodemus that a man must experience a supernatural birth if he is to enter God's supernatural Kingdom. This does not mean that God wants us to be mindless. But no man has ever thought his way into God's Kingdom. A learned theologian may be very knowledgeable about the Scriptures, church history or Christian doctrine and yet not know the reality of the Kingdom in his life. For receiving the gift of the Kingdom does not depend upon his knowledge, but on repentance and faith, leading to new birth.

To have faith in Jesus is actually to have our thinking enlarged, not diminished. Our minds need to be submitted to God's authority along with every other area of our lives, so that He can expand our thinking to embrace His supernatural thoughts. God is not irrational or unreasonable; He is simply beyond reason. Our rational thoughts cannot contain Him. That is why the Scriptures are a constant challenge to our faith; some of the things God says seem outrageously impossible. Yet we discover that when we apply faith to the Word, what He says proves true and what He promises comes to pass.

The Kingdom Jesus offers is a supernatural Kingdom. When arrested, Jesus made it clear; 'My kingdom is not of this world.' (John 18: 36) It comes from another place beyond the natural world. But He teaches us to pray: 'Your kingdom come, your will be done on earth as it is in heaven.' (Matt. 6: 10)

It is God's purpose that His supernatural Kingdom be spread in this natural world. Wherever Jesus is allowed to reign in the hearts and lives of His people, there His Kingdom is established and His will can be performed. It is there that His supernatural working will be in evidence. And that supernatural activity begins in the act of new birth, but is manifested in many other ways as Jesus demonstrates in His earthly ministry. The life of the believer is to be filled with God's supernatural activity and the Christian has available to him the infinite resources of God's power.

THE KINGDOM FIRST

Jesus goes on to teach His listeners not to be worried about their lives, their needs or the details of their circumstances. Rather 'seek first his kingdom and his righteousness, and all these things will be given to you as well.' (Matt. 6: 33)

The Kingdom is to be your priority. To seek first the Kingdom means that the heavenly King has pre-eminence in your life. You are no longer in bondage to your past, neither do you have to allow your life to be dominated by adverse circumstances. Your heavenly Father sees you living in His Son. He does not regard you, or deal with you, as if you are separate from Him. You are a child of His Kingdom; you belong to Him and He lives in you.

Every need will be met for those who put God's Kingdom and righteousness first – that is what Jesus promises. They do not have to be anxious about tomorrow. They do not need to be concerned about whether they will have enough to eat or wear. The Christian is to live as a child of the King, with the purposes of His Kingdom the priority in his life. He is to live in a position of righteousness before God, and is therefore to live in righteous ways each day of his life. When he falls into sin, the believer needs to be cleansed afresh by his Lord.

If the Christian entrusts himself to the King, desiring His purposes first, then the King will care for him in every detail. He can be confident that: 'In all things God works for the good of those who love him, who have been called according to his purpose.' (Rom. 8: 28) Christ will lead him in His triumphal procession, teaching him that mountains of need are to be moved and tossed in the sea; that nothing is impossible for the one who has faith in Jesus. Such victory is implied in living as a child of the Kingdom of God. For wherever the truth, the power and authority of His Kingdom is brought to bear, deception, need and rebellion are overcome.

So Jesus's simple, direct promise to those who believe in Him is: 'Ask and it will be given to you; seek and you will find; knock and the door will be opened to you. For everyone who asks receives; he who seeks finds; and to him who knocks, the door will be opened.' (Matt. 7: 7–8)

However, Jesus also makes it clear: 'Not everyone who says to me, "Lord, Lord," will enter the kingdom of heaven, but only he who does the will of my Father who is in heaven.' (Matt. 7: 21) Acknowledgment that Jesus is Lord is not the same as submission to Him as Lord in your life. It is the latter which concerns Jesus. Mighty things could be accomplished in the name of Jesus, for that name is greater than any other name and has power over all things. But Jesus will only recognise those who personally submit to His rule and reign in their lives; those who live as the children of the Kingdom. 'Many will say to me on that day, "Lord, Lord, did we not prophesy in your name, and in your name drive out demons and perform many miracles?" Then I will tell them plainly, "I never knew you. Away from me, you evildoers!"' (Matt. 7: 22–3)

To live as a child of the Kingdom is to do the will of the heavenly Father and that means putting God's Word into practice. The house built on sand could not withstand the storm. Jesus describes the man who built there as foolish. 'Everyone who hears these words of mine and does not put them into practice is like a foolish man who built his house on sand.' (Matt. 7: 26)

By contrast the wise man builds his house on rock; he hears the words of Jesus and puts them into practice. No matter how great the difficulties he encounters, his house proves to be unshakeable.

Those who have received the Kingdom have received a Kingdom that cannot be shaken. As the believer lives in the power of that positive Kingdom, he will not be shaken neither will he fall. The children of His Kingdom do not need to fear the power of the negative kingdom of darkness, for He who lives in them is greater than he who lives in the world. As their light shines before men, so the light of Christ can penetrate spiritual darkness and others can be brought into the glorious liberty of the sons of God.

Chapter 5

ETERNAL LIFE

In his account of the gospel, John rarely uses the phrase 'Kingdom of God'. Instead he speaks of the gift of eternal life, God's gift to those who believe, who are the children of God's Kingdom. He sent His Son that men might receive this gift: 'For God so loved the world that he gave his one and only Son, that whoever believes in him shall not perish but have eternal life.' (John 3: 16)

Those who reject Him 'perish', condemned by their own unbelief: 'Whoever believes in him is not condemned, but whoever does not believe stands condemned already because he has not believed in the name of God's one and only Son.' (v. 18)

'Whoever believes in the Son has eternal life, but whoever rejects the Son will not see life, for God's wrath remains on him.' (John 3: 36) Jesus speaks of eternal life as a present reality rather than a future hope – for the believer. Those who are thirsty for the reality of God in their lives will come to Him and find that He alone can give the water that will satisfy their thirst. 'Whoever drinks the water I give him will never thirst. Indeed, the water I give him will become in him a spring of water welling up to eternal life.' (John 4: 14) 'He who comes to me will never go hungry, and he who believes in me will never be thirsty.' (John 6: 35)

The one who hears the words of Jesus and believes His Father 'has eternal life and will not be condemned; he has crossed over from death to life.' (John 5: 24)

Knowing the Scriptures is not sufficient to give anyone this life. That was the mistake the Pharisees made. Jesus told them: 'You diligently study the Scriptures because you think that by them you possess eternal life. These are the Scriptures that testify about me, yet you refuse to come to me to have life.' (vv. 39–40)

In the same way, knowing the words and parables of the Kingdom does not make anyone a child of the Kingdom, or enable him to live in the power and authority of that Kingdom. He has to believe the Word and surrender his life to the King, before the Kingdom can be a reality in his experience.

Jesus told the people: 'Do not work for food that spoils, but for food that endures to eternal life, which the Son of Man will give you.' (John 6: 27) In other words, seek first the Kingdom of God and His righteousness and all that you need will be given you by Him. 'The work of God is this: to believe in the one he has sent.' (v. 29)

EVERLASTING KINGDOM

To those who receive God's gift of eternal life now, there is the promise of resurrection: 'For my Father's will is that everyone who looks to the Son and believes in him shall have eternal life, and I will raise him up at the last day.' (John 6: 40) The Kingdom Jesus came to give is eternal. In the prophecy of Daniel, we read: 'His kingdom is an eternal kingdom; his dominion endures from generation to generation.' (Dan. 4: 3) 'His kingdom will not be destroyed, his dominion will never end.' (Dan. 6: 26) And there is the glorious promise: 'The saints of the Most High will receive the kingdom and will possess it for ever – yes, for ever and ever.' (Dan. 7: 18)

The saints, those who have been redeemed by Jesus, can look forward to the final manifestation of the Kingdom in its fullness: 'Then the sovereignty, power and greatness of the kingdoms under the whole heaven will be handed over to the saints, the people of the Most High. His kingdom will be an everlasting kingdom, and all rulers will worship and obey him.' (Dan. 7: 27)

Over and over again Jesus impresses on His hearers the truth: 'He who believes has everlasting life.' (John 6: 47) 'Whoever eats my flesh and drinks my blood has eternal life, and I will raise him up at the last day.' (v. 54)

The disciples recognised that He had the words of eternal life. Those who kept His words would never see death. (John 8: 51) Jesus said that He came to give men life in all its fullness – not human life, for they already have that; but God's divine life, eternal life. Paul says: 'You have been given fullness in Christ.' (Col. 2: 10)

When speaking of Himself as the Good Shepherd, Jesus says: 'My sheep listen to my voice; I know them, and they follow me. I give them eternal life, and they shall never perish; no-one can snatch them out of my hand.' (John 10: 27–8) Again we notice the present reality of the gift of eternal life and also the fact that those who receive the gift are prepared to follow Him. 'His command leads to eternal life.' (John 12: 50) God does not give Himself to His children so that they may continue to pursue their own ways, but to follow Him along His way.

When praying before His arrest, Jesus said: 'Now this is eternal life: that they may know you, the only true God, and Jesus Christ, whom you have sent.' (John 17: 3) There is no other way to the Kingdom, to receiving the gift of eternal life, than through Him.

From this scriptural evidence we can see clearly that those who receive the gift of eternal life can expect to experience resurrection and the glory of God's Kingdom eternally. Paul speaks of what this means in 1 Corinthians 15.

RESURRECTION

The natural body is perishable, but there is also a spiritual body which is imperishable. The natural came first, then the spiritual. Adam signifies natural man, while Christ is the man of the Spirit. Natural men follow after Adam, while 'those who are of heaven' are as 'the man from heaven'. Those who have faith in Jesus 'bear the likeness of the man from heaven'.

Paul makes it clear that 'flesh and blood cannot inherit the kingdom of God, nor does the perishable inherit the imperishable.' (v. 50) Natural man cannot inherit the Kingdom; he must experience a supernatural, spiritual rebirth. He must become spiritual in order to enter the spiritual Kingdom of God.

God is in the business of transforming us into His likeness. But there will come the moment of complete change: 'Listen, I tell you a mystery: We will not all sleep but we will all be changed – in a flash, in the twinkling of an eye, at the last trumpet. For the trumpet will sound, the dead will be raised imperishable, and we will be changed.' (vv. 51–2) The perishable will then be clothed with the imperishable, and what is mortal with immortality. Death itself will have been defeated for the children of the Kingdom. 'But thanks be to God! He gives us the victory through our Lord Jesus Christ.' (v. 57)

And so Paul advises the Corinthians to stand firm and let nothing move them from their faith in Jesus and obedience to Him. They are always to give themselves to the Lord's work, confident that their labour in the Lord is not in vain. It will reap an everlasting reward. Jesus will reign until He has put all His enemies under His feet. Then He will hand over the Kingdom to His Father. Every negative dominion, authority and power will then have been destroyed.

In Revelation we read of those who have been purchased for God by the blood of Jesus: 'You have made them to be a kingdom and priests to serve our God, and they will reign on the earth.' (Rev. 5: 10) They will share in His exalted reign. Then the vision John had will be fulfilled: 'The kingdom of the world has become the kingdom of our Lord and of his

Christ, and he will reign for ever and ever.' (Rev. 11: 15)

When writing his first Epistle, John said: 'God has given us eternal life, and this life is in his Son. He who has the Son has life; he who does not have the Son of God does not have life.' (1 John 5: 11–12) And Paul urges Timothy to 'take hold of the eternal life to which you were called'. (1 Tim. 6: 12)

By the atoning work of Jesus we have been set free from sin and have become 'slaves to God', Paul tells the Romans. (6: 22) The benefit you reap, he says, leads to holiness, and the result is eternal life.

As those who inherit the Kingdom, we need to live as the children of the King *now*. As those who inherit eternal life, we need to live His life *now*. He gives us the Holy Spirit to enable us to do that. As we seek to follow His leading lovingly and obediently, we can live in the peace of God, confident of our heavenly destiny.

In the New Testament these two aspects of the Kingdom and God's gift of eternal life are held together. Both are a present reality for believers and, at the same time, a future hope, when they will know fully what is only experienced partially at present.

'The wages of sin is death, but the gift of God is eternal life in Christ Jesus our Lord.' (Rom. 6: 23) That gift is received by grace, by God's free gift; and it is by the continuing work of grace in the Christian's life that he lives in union with the will and purpose of Jesus. 'The one who sows to please the Spirit, from the Spirit will reap eternal life.' (Gal. 6: 8)

Chapter 6

THE SEED OF THE KINGDOM

SECRETS REVEALED

Jesus never taught without using parables. These parables of the Kingdom could be understood by some but not by others, which prompted the disciples to ask Jesus: 'Why do you speak to the people in parables?' (Matt. 13: 10)

Perhaps they were politely suggesting that Jesus should improve His teaching methods; after all, a good teacher can surely be understood by those he is teaching! Certainly they were genuinely perplexed themselves, making it necessary for Jesus to explain the parables to them.

His answer to their question is highly significant: 'The knowledge of the secrets of the kingdom of heaven has been given to you, but not to them.' (Matt. 13: 11) It seems that Jesus did not intend that everyone should understand His teaching on the Kingdom.

REVELATION

The secrets of the Kingdom of heaven can only be made known through revelation. They cannot be understood by reason alone. Not everybody is able to receive such revelation. To understand he is a child of the Kingdom, with all the resources of heaven available to him, places within a man's reach such infinite power and riches that can only be entrusted to those who are prepared to submit their lives to the King. Such resources cannot be made available to those who would abuse such gifts.

The presence of God's Kingdom on earth is a complete mystery to the vast majority of the population. There are many Christians even, who have never received the revelation in their hearts that they are children of the Kingdom, with God's infinite resources available to them.

Revelation of the Kingdom comes to a man in proportion to his willingness to submit to the authority of the King. The more submitted a man, the more Kingdom power and authority can radiate from his life. God's intention is that there should be progressive revelation of the truth of the Kingdom in a Christian's life that will lead to a progressive increase in spiritual power and authority, in faith and the manifestation of Jesus in his life.

It is for this reason that Jesus continues His answer to the disciples' question about why He uses parables, by saying: 'Whoever has will be given more, and he will have an abundance. Whoever does not have, even what he has will be taken from him.' (Matt. 13: 12)

At first this might seem unjust. But it is God's purpose that each of His children should experience His abundance in their lives. That means that they receive from God all they need and more. They have more than enough of His resources for themselves spiritually and materially, and are enabled to express His generosity by the way in which they give to others.

Whoever has the Kingdom as a gift from God will experience the Lord pouring His riches abundantly into his life, as he continues to seek first the Kingdom of God and His righteousness. Whoever does not have the Kingdom as a gift will ultimately experience what he has being taken from him.

This is a hard truth to face. Jesus made it clear to the Jews that, although as God's chosen people they should have been the ones to inherit the Kingdom, many Gentiles would be preferred before them. Those who by virtue of their birth should be the children of the Kingdom will instead be thrown out because of their rejection of the King, their Messiah: 'I say to you that many will come from the east and the west, and will take their places at the feast with Abraham, Isaac and Jacob in the kingdom of heaven. But the subjects of the kingdom will be thrown outside, into the darkness, where there will be weeping and gnashing of teeth.' (Matt. 8: 11–12)

Jesus is the only Saviour; He is the Way, the Truth and the Life, and no-one will come into the Kingdom of His Father except through Him.

Evangelism is always the priority of the Church, and that often needs to begin with those already sitting in the pews on Sundays. Judgment begins with the household of God. He expects great things of those who claim to be His people and gives mighty promises to those who genuinely are His children. It is not a question of calling Him 'Lord' but of doing His will, of living lives submitted to Him as King.

Those who do not belong to His Kingdom see and yet do not see; they hear but do not understand the revelation of the Kingdom. But to the believing disciples Jesus says: 'But blessed are your eyes because they see, and your ears because they hear. For I tell you the truth, many prophets and righteous men longed to see what you see but did not see it, and to hear what you hear but did not hear it.' (Matt. 13: 16–17)

Even the men of God who preceded Jesus were not able to receive the gift that is offered through Jesus. This is true even of John the Baptist who was sent to prepare the way for the ministry of Jesus, with his call to repentance and righteousness. Jesus said: 'I tell you the truth: Among those born of women there has not risen anyone greater than John the Baptist; yet he who is least in the Kingdom of heaven is greater than he.' (Matt. 11: 11)

What a privilege to be a child of the Kingdom! To belong to the Kingdom of God raises a person above his natural heritage. For the Kingdom of God is supernatural and when a person is born again, God's supernatural activity gives him supernatural life; he possesses eternal life. Those from former generations found righteous by God will enjoy His heavenly inheritance. But none of them, neither the prophets nor John the Baptist, could experience the Kingdom of God NOW, could enter that Kingdom NOW, receive the benefits of that Kingdom NOW. That only became possible when Jesus, the King of heaven, came to dwell among men with His sovereign call: 'Repent, for the kingdom of heaven is near.' (Matt. 4: 17)

John the Baptist had spoken these same words (Matt. 3: 2). On his lips they were pregnant with significance, for they proclaimed that the King was about to come. On the lips of Jesus they are even more significant. The King has come and now the Kingdom is made available to those who believe in Him. The Baptist willingly makes way for the Messiah.

THE SOWER

In His parables of the Kingdom Jesus often used examples of growth. No parable is better known than that of the Sower. The farmer sows seed which falls on four different types of ground. Some falls on the path, where it is eaten by birds. Some falls on rocky places where the plants wither when the sun scorches them, because they have no depth to their roots. Other seed falls among thorns which choke the plants; but other falls on good soil producing a crop – a hundred, sixty or thirty times what was sown.

It was after hearing this that the disciples put their question to Jesus about why He should speak in parables. He explained that the seed represents the Word or gospel of the Kingdom. There is nothing wrong with the seed; it is the same wherever it falls. It is the quality of the ground that is different.

THE PATH

The path, Jesus says, represents the one who 'hears the message about the kingdom and does not understand it'. He does not receive the revelation that is given to him. So 'the evil one comes and snatches away what was sown in his heart.' (Matt. 13: 19) Satan is represented in the parable by the birds that eat the seed.

Those represented by the path do actually hear the message of the Kingdom; God sows the Word in their hearts. They are given revelation but they reject it. 'Satan comes and takes away the word that was sown in them.' (Mark 4: 15). 'The devil comes and takes away the word from their hearts, so that they cannot believe and be saved.' (Luke 8: 12)

Satan obviously is concerned that people should not receive the message of the Kingdom. This is hardly surprising. Until a man believes and is saved he belongs to Satan's domain, the kingdom of darkness; he is still spiritually blinded by the god of this age. The enemy wants to hold on to those he controls, whether they recognise the reality of that control or not. He knows that as soon as a man responds with repentance and faith to the revelation that God is offering to give him the Kingdom of Light, he will lose control over that individual. Until his conversion, Satan is able to manipulate that person.

When a man responds to the gospel, he becomes part of that Kingdom from which Satan has been dismissed. This fact not only fills the enemy with envy but also with fear. Jesus explains why. To those who are part of the Kingdom He has given 'authority to trample on snakes and scorpions, and to overcome all the power of the enemy'. (Luke 10: 19) Nothing will harm them.

We can see why Satan has such a vested interest in trying to prevent people from receiving the revelation of the Kingdom. Whereas formerly he was able to control and manipulate the unbeliever, encouraging him to deny the lordship of Jesus in his life and urging him to live by his own natural powers and resources, now the roles are reversed. The believer is not only delivered from the domain of darkness and Satan's control; he is given power and authority to overcome all the power of the enemy. Whereas before Satan could constantly defeat him, even without him being aware of his influence, now the Christian can inflict one defeat after another on Satan.

Jesus explains to the disciples why this is: 'Your names are written in heaven.' In other words, they belong to the Kingdom of which Satan is no longer a part. Instead of fearing his influence, they can now rise up in victory over him. For wherever Light shines, the darkness has to disappear. They should rejoice, not so much in the victories themselves, as in the reason for them: 'Your names are written in heaven.' (Luke 10: 20) Not will be written, but already are written! The authority of heaven is already available to those who believe and are part of God's Kingdom.

So if the enemy can prevent someone from responding to the initial revelation of the Kingdom, he will most certainly do so. He does not like to lose control of people's lives and suffer defeat.

THE ROCKY SOIL

The rocky places represent 'the man who hears the word and at once receives it with joy. But since he has no root, he lasts only a short time. When trouble or persecution comes because of the word, he quickly falls away.' (Matt. 13: 20–1)

This man receives the revelation of the Kingdom with joy. How wonderful that God, the Almighty Creator, should love him, be prepared to forgive him all his sins and make him an inheritor of the Kingdom of heaven. He responds positively to the revelation, but his life is not deeply rooted in the Word of God. He is the one who clamours for experiences of the Lord, but does not know how to live as a child of the Kingdom. He does not know the rights God gives him, or the power and authority that are vested in him.

Because he is not a man of the Word, when he is in the middle of adverse circumstances he does not know how to cope. He believes his feelings and fears, rather than the truth of God's Word. 'In the time of testing they fall away.' (Luke 8: 13)

It is not enough to receive the gift of the Kingdom. Every child of God needs to learn how to live Kingdom life, exercise Kingdom authority, have Kingdom faith and enjoy Kingdom victories. But he will only be able to do all this if his life is deeply rooted in Kingdom words; if he believes the gospel of the Kingdom and puts those words into practice. Then his house will be built on rock, not sand, and will withstand any storm.

THE THORNY SOIL

The thorns represent those who hear the Word, which begins to be rooted in their lives and to grow in them, but who allow other things to choke their spiritual growth, making them unfruitful. They do not mature as Christians.

Fruitfulness and maturity are God's purpose for all His children. To receive the gift of the Kingdom is only the beginning of His purpose for the believer. 'You did not choose me, but I chose you to go and bear fruit – fruit that will last', Jesus tells His disciples. (John 15: 16) He calls us not only to enjoy the benefits of the Kingdom but to bear fruit for His glory: 'This is to my Father's glory, that you bear much fruit, showing yourselves to be my disciples.' (John 15: 8)

Paul urges his readers to 'become mature'. Spiritual maturity is dependent on the Christian allowing the Word of God to be increasingly expressed in his life through the enabling of the Holy Spirit.

Jesus says there are three things in particular that prevent fruitfulness and the believer becoming mature.

1. The worries of this life. Nothing hinders faith more than

anxiety. Worry demonstrates that the person is failing to trust God in those particular circumstances. He believes the problems rather than the Lord. In effect his attitude is: 'God can't handle the situation, so I shall worry about it!'

Jesus clearly says that if the Kingdom is first in your life and you are seeking to live in righteousness, then you need have no worries or be anxious about anything. Even if your immediate reaction to a difficult situation is to be fearful, you can confess the sin of that negative reaction and entrust the whole matter to the Lord. He is able to cope with every circumstance and promises to give you everything you need.

Worry, fear and anxiety are all negative and do not, therefore, belong to the positive Kingdom of God. They emanate from the negative domain of darkness and are encouraged by the prince of this world. During our years of unbelief many of us become accustomed to being worriers, meeting every difficulty with anxiety. This is not Kingdom living. We cannot live in victory over our circumstances if we constantly worry about them.

2. 'The deceitfulness of wealth' is another thorn that chokes the life of the Kingdom in a believer.

Jesus was to tell His disciples: 'I tell you the truth, it is hard for a rich man to enter the kingdom of heaven. Again I tell you, it is easier for a camel to go through the eye of a needle than for a rich man to enter the kingdom of God.' (Matt. 19: 23–4)

Jesus is talking here of *entering* the Kingdom. It is hard for rich people to *enter* the Kingdom. Those who have no material need are usually in love with the things of this world, and have no time or place for God. Certainly most wealthy people do not want to submit themselves to the authority of Another, albeit the Son of God. Each wants to reign in his own little kingdom.

That is true for many who would not be described as 'wealthy', but who are by no means impoverished. Pride encourages any person stubbornly to refuse to submit to the authority of Jesus. Wealth easily enhances such pride.

It is hard for a rich man to enter the Kingdom because he is unlikely to see the need to do so. He has all he wants to fulfil his ambition and probably does not want the course of his life to be changed by anyone, even God.

Jesus does not preach against wealth as such; neither does He say it is impossible for rich people to become part of His Kingdom. He is simply stating that much is stacked against them, for the flesh is opposed to the Spirit and it is so easy to indulge the flesh when wealthy.

There are many fine Christians who are wealthy people. Their lives have been submitted to the King and Jesus is therefore allowed to rule over their finances. He teaches: 'Give, and it will be given to you. A good measure, pressed down, shaken together and running over, will be poured into your lap. For with the measure you use, it will be measured to you.' (Luke 6: 38)

This is a spiritual principle that relates to many areas of our lives, irrespective of our material resources. It is true of forgiveness, for example. If we forgive others their sins, God will be willing to forgive us. If we do not judge we shall not be judged. If we do not condemn, we shall not be condemned.

The same principle applies to money. If we honour God in our giving (no matter the level of our wealth), He will cause us to prosper materially. He is no man's debtor and will always measure back to us more than is freely, willingly and joyfully given to Him.

Jesus says that it is the *deceitfulness* of wealth that will choke the life of the Kingdom in a believer. Money encourages deceit. Many (not only the wealthy) desire to hide the amount they possess from tax officers, neighbours and fellow Christians. It is considered a very private area of our lives.

As Christians we should have nothing to hide. We should not be ashamed of others knowing what we possess, or what we give for the work of the Kingdom, although Jesus warns us not to parade our giving before others.

The devil is the deceiver. Deceit does not belong in the lives of the children of light. Wealth itself is not necessarily evil; it is the love of money that is the root of all evil. It is the misuse of our wealth, using it for our own ends rather than to serve God, that chokes Kingdom growth in our lives.

We are to honour God in our giving. The tithe is rightfully His; that is, the first tenth of all we have or earn. It is His by right and is to be given to Him for the use of His Kingdom. Over and above that we make our free-will offerings.

The first tenth is a minimum, for the Christian acknowledges that all he is and has rightly belongs to the Lord. Giving the tithe faithfully is a necessary indication that we are truly submitted to the authority of God in our lives. We are ready to give generously to the One who has given His everything for us and to us.

Our money is Kingdom money, and we are not to try and hide it deceitfully from the Lord. When you desire to serve the King with your finances, He knows He can cause you to prosper so that more resources can be released through you for the work of the Kingdom.

It matters, therefore, where you give as well as what you give. Because your money is Kingdom money, what is given away needs to be used for the work and extension of the Kingdom. Paul teaches that the man who sows sparingly will reap sparingly, and the one who sows plentifully will reap plentifully. The nature of the soil into which the seed is sown is also of vital importance. There is no point in sowing good seed in a spiritual desert, on a path, rocky soil or among thorns. Sow it in good soil where you know it will be productive.

3. 'Desires for other things' also choke the life of the Kingdom. Wealth can encourage such desires; but those who are without can be full of envy and greed also.

The Kingdom must remain first in the Christian's life. That will only be a reality if he places the King Himself at the centre of his life.

Some claim to have a close and loving relationship with the Lord but care little for His Kingdom. They are deceived. To care for the King is to care for what He counts dear. He wants to see His Kingdom come and His will done on earth as in heaven. 'If you love me, you will obey what I command', Jesus said. (John 14: 15) Obedience is submission to the will and authority of God out of love for Him. If the motive is love, it will not be a begrudging obedience or submission, but a joyful one.

Nothing, or nobody, comes before the Lord in our lives. Putting anything or anyone before Him stifles the growth of Kingdom life within us. We cannot be seeking first the Kingdom and putting other desires first at the same time.

The Christian, therefore, yields his independence to the Lord. He no longer wants his life ruled by selfish ambition, but by the Word and Spirit of God. He cannot seek his own ends and God's purposes at the same time. All that matters to him, if he is to be increasingly fruitful, is that God should be glorified in his life by His purpose being fulfilled in him.

THE GOOD SOIL

The good soil represents those who hear the Word of the Kingdom with an honest and good heart, and retain it. They hold fast to that Word; they keep it; they live it. Because they live as Kingdom children they are fruitful, 'yielding a hundred, sixty or thirty times what was sown.' (Matt. 13: 23)

The capacity for each may differ, but God's purpose is that each of His children should increase in fruitfulness. 'Every branch that does bear fruit he trims clean so that it will be even more fruitful.' (John 15: 2) The Father cuts out of our lives the things that are negative, so that more of the positive life of His Kingdom may be manifested in us.

If God chooses to give us His Kingdom, which is positive, how is it that so many negative things can persist in our lives? These negatives obviously hinder fruitfulness.

Many of these parables of the Kingdom are parables of growth. We cannot grow to the point where we receive the Kingdom; that is God's gift to those who repent and believe. But this gift of the Kingdom is like a seed that God plants in the heart and life of that believer.

Like all natural seeds, the seed of the Kingdom contains all the life that will potentially develop out of it. The seed needs the right soil in order to grow to maturity and fruitfulness; it also needs to be watered spiritually.

Jesus describes the Holy Spirit as 'living water'. The seed of the Kingdom planted in the life of the believer is watered by the Holy Spirit. Having given the gift of the Kingdom, God does not tell the new Christian to try his hardest to live as a child of the Kingdom. His own natural resources are inadequate to enable him to do so.

God gives you His Holy Spirit to enable you to live the life of His Kingdom here on earth. He asks nothing of you without supplying all the grace and resources to fulfil His purposes. The living water of the Holy Spirit waters the seed of the Kingdom within you, enabling its life to grow within you.

This is a progressive work and as you continue to allow the Holy Spirit to water the seed it will become a shoot, then a plant that will mature and become fruitful. And a fruitful plant reproduces a number of identical seeds to that from which it came. Fruitfulness produces 'a crop, yielding a hundred, sixty or thirty times *what was sown.*'

'What was sown' was the seed of the Kingdom; it produces Kingdom seeds. In other words the presence of the Kingdom within you will influence others to seek first the Kingdom of God and His righteousness. Every Christian should have a great desire to see the life of the Kingdom reproduced in others. God gives His Holy Spirit that you will have the power to be a witness of the Kingdom in the world.

It is for this reason that, in His great prayer recorded in John 17, Jesus says: 'As you sent me into the world, I have sent them into the world.' (John 17: 18) You are a witness of the presence of God's Kingdom in the world. Your citizenship is now in heaven and there will come the time when you will be able to enjoy His heavenly glory without the temptations of the world, the flesh and the devil. Until then you resist these temptations and become increasingly fruitful by living Kingdom life in the world, with a heart full of enthusiasm and zeal that God will use you to spread the influence of His Kingdom.

Chapter 7

KINGDOM GROWTH

WEEDS

Another Kingdom parable of growth is that of the Weeds. A man sowed good seed in his field. 'But while everyone was sleeping, his enemy came and sowed weeds among the wheat, and went away.' (Matt. 13: 25) Both the wheat and weeds grew together.

The man's servant suggested that the weeds be pulled up. But the master said 'No' to this suggestion 'because while you are pulling the weeds, you may root up the wheat with them.' (v. 29) Both were to be allowed to grow together until harvest time. The harvesters will be told: 'First collect the weeds and tie them in bundles to be burned, then gather the wheat and bring it into my barn.' (v. 30)

Like that of the Sower, this parable also had to be explained privately by Jesus to the disciples. The one who sowed the good seed is the Son of Man, Jesus Himself. The field is the world and the good seed are the sons of the Kingdom. Jesus has sown the seed of the Kingdom in the world and those who have responded to His gospel grow like the wheat towards fruitfulness.

But the devil has also sown his negative seeds, and Jesus describes the weeds as 'the sons of the evil one'.

The servant wants to do away with the evil ones so that the good seed will be unhindered in its growth. This, however, is not God's way. The servant may uproot good seed in his zeal to do away with all those who are evil. New birth turns what was formerly a weed into a stalk of wheat! God alone knows the heart of each individual and the time will come when the fruitfulness (either positive or negative) of each person's life will be obvious.

The harvest time, Jesus says, is the end of the age, when He will send out the harvesters who are His angels. We should note carefully the sequence of events as Jesus explains them.

First the angels 'will weed out of his kingdom everything that causes sin and all who do evil. They will throw them into the fiery furnace, where there will be weeping and gnashing of teeth.' (vv. 41–2)

It seems, at first sight, that those who cause sin and do evil are actually part of the Kingdom. But this is not the case. At the end of the age, the sovereignty of Jesus will suddenly be established everywhere. Every knee will have to bow before Jesus and every tongue will have to confess that He is Lord.

But those who have resisted His gospel and have remained in their sins will not be able to stand this day of His coming. For them, this is the time of judgment and the angels of God will swiftly root them out of the Kingdom. They will be condemned to a Christless eternity, separated from God. Hell is described as the 'fiery furnace, where there will be weeping and gnashing of teeth.'

By contrast Jesus teaches: 'I tell you the truth, whoever hears my word and believes him who sent me has eternal life and will not be condemned; he has crossed over from death to life.' (John 5: 24)

What a contrast! There is no condemnation for those who are in Christ Jesus. By their faith in Him crucified, they have already been raised to new life, have received the gift of eternal life and are children of God's Kingdom.

As Jesus concludes this parable He says that 'the righteous will shine like the sun in the kingdom of their Father.' (Matt. 13: 43) Is it not worth seeking first His Kingdom and righteousness?

MADE PERFECT

As you remain faithful to the end, you will be numbered among those made righteous through the blood of Jesus. You will be so radiant with the reflected glory of God that no human eye could look at you. You will shine like the sun in the Kingdom of your Father, in that Kingdom of which you are already a part, but which has only been imperfectly manifested in you and around you.

'But when perfection comes, the imperfect disappears.' (1 Cor. 13: 10) Not only will unforgiven sinners be rooted out and condemned to hell, the final refining of the saints of God will take place in the twinkling of an eye.

> So will it be with the resurrection of the dead. The body that is sown is perishable, it is raised imperishable; it is sown in dishonour, it is raised in glory; it is sown in weakness, it is raised in power; it is sown a natural body, it is raised a spiritual body . . . as is the man from heaven, so also are those who are of heaven. And just as we have borne the likeness of the earthly man, so shall we bear the likeness of the man from heaven. I declare to you, brothers, that flesh and blood cannot inherit the kingdom of God, nor does the perishable inherit the imperishable. Listen, I tell you a mystery: We will not all sleep, but we will all be changed – in a flash, in the twinkling of an eye, at the last trumpet. For the trumpet will sound, the dead will be raised imperishable, and we will be changed . . . But thanks be to God! He gives us the victory through our Lord Jesus Christ. (1 Cor. 15: 42–4, 48–52, 57)

Paul is addressing Christians when writing these words. Although they have entered into their inheritance of God's Kingdom because of His precious and gracious gift to them, they can long for the full manifestation of that Kingdom when Christ returns, not as a humble servant, but as the reigning King.

Then all who have denied His sovereignty will pass away, but those who have acknowledged His lordship and lived under His reign will know this glorious transformation. Death has lost its sting and they are given the victory over it through Jesus.

The glorious promise that we have as the King's children is that, when we see Him face to face, we shall be like Him. God's purpose for us will be fulfilled. He gives us the gift of His *Holy* Spirit to make us holy, like Him, and to bring us to that perfection which is His plan for us.

THE MUSTARD SEED AND THE YEAST

Both these short parables of the Kingdom speak to us of growth. 'The kingdom of heaven is like a mustard seed, which a man took and planted in his field. Though it is the smallest of all your seeds, yet when it grows, it is the largest of the garden plants and becomes a tree, so that the birds of the air come and perch in its branches.' (Matt. 13: 31-2)

There is both an individual and a corporate sense in which we can understand this parable. At the personal level, God has planted the seed of His Kingdom in the lives of those who believe in Him. As that seed is watered by the Holy Spirit, so it will grow to maturity and become fruitful. What started as a tiny seed in the new-born Christian becomes a 'tree' that can minister to others in the world.

Corporately, the Kingdom of God on earth seems tiny and perhaps insignificant to the great majority of people. Nevertheless, throughout the world that Kingdom is being extended every day and in due course its power and influence will overshadow everything else. There will be times of great spiritual conflict on earth before Christ finally returns in glory. But God's Kingdom will prevail; it is the unshakeable Kingdom.

Meanwhile the children of the Kingdom are like yeast: 'The kingdom of heaven is like yeast that a woman took and mixed into a large amount of flour until it worked all through the dough.' (Matt. 13: 33)

God's Kingdom people seem a tiny minority of the world's population. Yet amid all the religions, philosophies and ideologies that exist, it is those Kingdom children who will finally prevail. Their lives are to be like yeast working through this large amount of flour, tiny and seemingly insignificant, yet powerful with the ability to change the world in which they live.

Individually, the message is consistent with the other Kingdom parables. Just as the seed is planted in the heart of the believer, so the life of the Kingdom within him is like the yeast that will spread its influence through every area of his being, so that every part of his life will be brought under the sovereignty of Jesus. His reign already established in him will progressively take a more complete hold on his life.

THE HIDDEN TREASURE AND THE PEARL

These two short parables speak of the inexpressible value of the Kingdom. 'The kingdom of heaven is like treasure hidden in a field. When a man found it, he hid it again, and then in his joy went and sold all he had and bought that field.' (Matt. 13: 44)

Jesus says the Kingdom is the treasure – not Himself. We cannot possess the Kingdom without submitting to the King. But God does not desire people to submit to Jesus without realising that they have been given a Kingdom to possess. Possessing that Kingdom is the treasure.

Again Jesus speaks here of the hidden nature of the Kingdom. It is present among men and yet unnoticed by most people. It requires revelation to understand that God is offering this Kingdom to those who repent and believe. Once a man sees what God is offering, it becomes supremely important to him that he obtains that Kingdom. All his

worldly possessions are insignificant by comparison.

Of course the Kingdom cannot be purchased, and Jesus does not mean to imply that it can. He simply makes clear that, once a man has received revelation of the Kingdom, his overwhelming desire will be to possess that Kingdom.

It is possible for someone to be a Christian for some time before receiving this heart-revelation. Jesus does not intend any believer to acknowledge Him as King without entering into this inheritance of the Kingdom. Even to the believer, it is like discovering treasure to realise suddenly that God has chosen to give him the Kingdom, that He has given him in Christ every spiritual blessing in heavenly places.

'Again, the kingdom of heaven is like a merchant looking for fine pearls. When he found one of great value, he went away and sold everything he had and bought it.' (Matt. 13: 45-6)

The message of this parable is similar. Like the merchant many today are searching. They see there must be a meaning and purpose to life, and feel a sense of emptiness and frustration because they have not found it.

Most try to create purpose for themselves, endeavouring to find happiness and fulfilment in a variety of ways. They may try the route of self-indulgence, seeking many fleshly pleasures for themselves. They may be so disillusioned with the world that they try to escape from reality through drugs or drink. They may try to find fulfilment through their work, devoting themselves to advancing in their chosen career, often regardless of other considerations.

They may even devote themselves to the welfare of others through various social activities. Yet none of these things can bring spiritual fulfilment or satisfaction. None can produce that peace which is beyond all understanding.

Like the merchant, a person's search for meaning and purpose only ends when he discovers the reality of the Kingdom of God. Then he knows he must become part of the Kingdom. Then he discovers that fleshly pleasures are illusory; ultimately they create more pain than pleasure. He no longer needs to try and escape from his circumstances through drugs or drink, for now he has within him the resources, not only to cope, but to be part of God's mission to extend His Kingdom in the world. From a position of passive defeat, he can move to one of active victory.

He will not try to lose himself in his career, for he desires only to please God by fulfilling the ministry and purpose to which He calls him. More than ever before, he will share God's love for people and will be concerned about their welfare. He will not only want to see the hungry fed and the homeless housed, he will be concerned for their spiritual welfare. He will want them, and indeed all men, to know the joy of discovering the Kingdom of heaven as a present reality.

Chapter 8

MANY CALLED, FEW CHOSEN

THE NET

A net was let down into the lake and caught all kinds of fish. When full, the fishermen hauled it to the shore, sat down and collected the good fish into baskets, but threw the bad away.

As with the parable of the Weeds, Jesus relates this to the end of the age. 'The angels will come and separate the wicked from the righteous and throw them into the fiery furnace, where there will be weeping and gnashing of teeth.' (Matt. 13: 49–50)

On this occasion Jesus asks His listeners if they have understood, and they reply affirmatively. It is not fashionable to talk or preach about hell today. When teaching about the Kingdom, Jesus did not want people to be under any illusion that 'everyone will be all right in the end'. There will be a judgment when the wicked will be consigned to hell. The righteous, those cleansed by the blood of Jesus and made righteous in God's sight, need not fear this judgment, for they have already passed from death to life.

To those who reject Jesus, as much by their apathy and indecision as by their down-right opposition, this judgment and its inevitable consequences will be an awful reality. 'He who is not with me is against me,' said Jesus. (Matt. 12: 30)

Every believer will have to give an account of his stewardship, of how he has used the Kingdom resources made available to him. This we shall see clearly in Kingdom parables Jesus taught later in His ministry. But the man who is assured of his salvation does not have to fear being condemned to hell.

Some question how a God of love could allow people to endure such an eternity. In His love He sent His Son to save men from such punishment, which they deserve because of their sin and rebellion against Him. In His love and mercy He has opened the way of salvation to them – not only by making provision to deliver them from all the negatives of sin, fear, unbelief and ultimate death, but also by offering them the positive gift of His Kingdom and pouring His own positive life into them through the Holy Spirit.

If some choose to reject what God offers, it is not He who condemns them; they condemn themselves. Jesus warns them that there will be inevitable consequences to their rejection of Him.

> Whoever believes in him is not condemned, but whoever does not believe stands condemned already because he has not believed in the name of God's one and only Son. This is the verdict: Light has come into the world, but men loved darkness instead of light because their deeds were evil. Everyone who does evil hates the light, and will not come into the light for fear that his deeds will be exposed. But whoever lives by the truth comes into the light, so that it may be seen plainly that what he has done has been done through God. (John 3: 18–21)

These words speak for themselves. But Jesus precedes these with the statement: 'God did not send his Son into the world to condemn the world, but to save the world through him.' (v. 17) That demonstrates the Father's heart and desire. The salvation He wants for the world is available 'through Him', through Jesus. To reject Jesus is to reject the only way of salvation. 'For my Father's will is that everyone who looks to the Son and believes in him shall have eternal life, and I will raise him up at the last day.' (John 6: 40)

A man's eternal destiny is dependent on whether he accepts or rejects Jesus; on whether he accepts God's offer of His Kingdom now or throws it back in His face. To reject the Kingdom in this life will lead to eternal exclusion from it.

Every Christian needs to sense the urgency of sharing his faith with non-believers. God calls him to do that, no matter what reaction he receives from others. It is not for us to judge the eternal destiny of any individual; only to make others aware of the gospel. God alone is the Judge.

Jesus will not come again until the nations have heard the gospel. But what of all those deceived by the world's false religions, or those who have never heard of Jesus? There are not many ways to the one God. The other major religions (Judaism apart) worship false gods and demonic spirits. Their adherents are tragically deceived. They live in the kingdom of darkness, for Christ alone can rescue men and transfer them to the Kingdom of Light.

UNDER JUDGMENT

For the ungodly, the consequences seem inevitable. Paul says: 'The wrath of God is being revealed from heaven against all the godlessness and wickedness of men who suppress the truth by their wickedness, since what may be known about God is plain to them, because God has made it plain to them.' (Rom. 1: 18–19)

There is ample evidence for the existence of God and He will be found by all who seek Him. There can be no excuse for unbelief in God; no excuse for not seeking Him. 'For since the creation of the world God's invisible qualities – his eternal power and divine nature – have been clearly seen, being understood from what has been made, so that men are without any excuse.' (Rom. 1: 20)

To know or believe there is a God does not mean that people will care about Him, seek His will, worship Him or

acknowledge Him in any other way. To believe in the
existence of God does not give anybody a ticket to heaven. All
have sinned and fallen short of God's glory, and will not be
restored to that glory without a Saviour.

When people chose to please themselves rather than obey
God, He 'gave them over in the sinful desires of their hearts to
sexual impurity for the degrading of their bodies with one
another. They exchanged the truth of God for a lie, and
worshipped and served created things rather than the
Creator.' (Rom. 1: 24–5) That is the sorry truth for many
brought up as children to believe in God, but who have
chosen to live in their own way instead of His.

> Furthermore, since they did not think it worth while to
> retain the knowledge of God, he gave them over to a
> depraved mind, to do what ought not to be done. They have
> become filled with every kind of wickedness, evil, greed
> and depravity. They are full of envy, murder, strife, deceit
> and malice. They are gossips, slanderers, God-haters,
> insolent, arrogant and boastful; they invent ways of doing
> evil; they disobey their parents; they are senseless,
> faithless, heartless, ruthless. Although they know God's
> righteous decree that those who do such things deserve
> death, they not only continue to do these very things
> but also approve of those who practise them. (Rom.
> 1: 28–32)

That is a very apt description of modern Western society. If
men choose to go their own way instead of His, He allows
them to do so. He will force nobody to obey Him. He desires
our love. He will not make us as robots programmed to do His
will, or puppets dancing because He pulls the string.

Paul continues: 'we know that God's judgment against
those who do such things is based on truth.' (Rom. 2: 2)
Because of the riches of His kindness, tolerance, patience and
love He leads men to repentance so that they might know the
joy of His Kingdom.

What of those who refuse to be so led, who seem to care nothing for the purposes of God? 'Because of your stubbornness and your unrepentant heart, you are storing up wrath against yourself for the day of God's wrath, when his righteous judgment will be revealed.' (Rom. 2: 5)

He will certainly deal justly with every man. 'God "will give to each person according to what he has done." To those who by persistence in doing good seek glory, honour and immortality, he will give eternal life. But for those who are self-seeking and who reject the truth and follow evil, there will be wrath and anger.' (Rom. 2: 6–8)

These are the two options open to every person. But Paul does make it clear that God will judge each according to the revelation he has received. 'All who sin apart from the law will also perish apart from the law, and all who sin under the law will be judged by the law. For it is not those who hear the law who are righteous in God's sight, but it is those who obey the law who will be declared righteous.' (Rom. 2: 12–13)

UNDER LAW

This, of course, refers to the Jewish law given by God through Moses. But what of those who come neither from a Jewish nor Christian background and who are ignorant of the real God? Paul says that even though they do not have God's law, some do by nature what the law requires. 'They are a law for themselves,' he says. 'They show that the requirements of the law are written on their hearts, their consciences also bearing witness, and their thoughts now accusing, now even defending them.' (vv. 14–15)

People will not be judged by the amount of revelation they have received, but by whether they have lived according to that revelation. This however falls far short of the glory God holds out to us through Jesus Christ. Through Him we can know forgiveness of sins, have peace with Him, assurance of our salvation and receive the gift of His Kingdom. God Himself comes to live in us by the power of the Holy Spirit

that we might know the glorious liberty of the sons of God NOW.

This revelation is far superior to any other, even that given by God to Moses. But if the revelation is greater, so is the responsibility to live in righteousness, loving and obeying our heavenly Father. The Christian is not, therefore, in the position of a judge of the eternal destiny of particular individuals. It is for him to ensure that he is being faithful, so that he may be most effective in his witness to those who do not know the truth.

Jesus says: 'every teacher of the law who has been instructed about the kingdom of heaven is like the owner of a house who brings out of his storeroom new treasures as well as old.' (Matt. 13: 52) Jesus came to fulfil the law, which reveals what God requires of His people. They are unable to fulfil His demands by their own efforts, or work their way to heaven by trying to be righteous. The Jews, like everyone else, needed the revelation of the Kingdom. Receiving the life and resources of that Kingdom makes obedience possible; God's purposes can then be fulfilled.

If he is wise, the Jew who has sought to keep the law of God will embrace what is newly revealed to him. The heavenly Father has supplied a Saviour, who has made it possible for him to be delivered from his sins, and receive the gift of His Kingdom. Now the Father wants to live in him by the Holy Spirit.

Then the believer can fulfil the law because he has already been made acceptable to God. He can worship and pray, not according to prescribed rites and ceremonies, but in the power of the Holy Spirit. He no longer has to strive to be worthy of entering the Kingdom of heaven. It is already his by God's gracious gift.

Chapter 9

GOD'S OPEN INVITATION

Jesus made it clear that it was never too late in this life to receive the Kingdom from God. However, the sooner a person inherits this glorious gift, the sooner he can live in the good of it. He will have the joy of serving the King in this life as well as reigning with Him eternally.

WORKERS IN THE VINEYARD

Jesus likened the Kingdom of heaven to a landowner who went out early in the morning to hire men to work in his vineyard. He agreed to pay them a denarius for their day's work. He went out again at the third hour to hire others promising, 'I will pay you whatever is right.' He did the same again at the sixth, ninth and even the eleventh hour.

When he paid their wages at the end of the day all received the same amount, whether they had been hired early or towards the end of the day. Some 'began to grumble against the landowner. "These men who were hired last worked only one hour," they said, "and you have made them equal to us who have borne the burden of the work and the heat of the day."' (Matt. 20: 11-12)

The landowner said he was not being unfair. They had agreed to work for a denarius and had received what was promised them. 'I want to give the man who was hired last the same as I gave you. Don't I have the right to do what I want with my own money? Or are you envious because I am generous?' (vv. 14–15)

Jesus is here revealing more of the nature of the King and, therefore, of His Kingdom. The Lord, represented by the landowner, is the one who calls people into His Kingdom at various stages of their lives. Some live a lifetime of devotion to the King, giving themselves wholeheartedly to the work of the Kingdom. Others repent and acknowledge His Lordship only late in their lives. Yet to all there is the same reward: they inherit the Kingdom of heaven. There can be no greater reward, neither can there be anything less because God has made His Kingdom available to all who repent and believe.

He does not make part of His Kingdom available to some and less of His Kingdom to others. His Kingdom is present where He rules and reigns, and the full privileges and resources of the Kingdom are made available to all Christians. The whole 'seed' is planted in every believer's life.

Those 'who have borne the burden of the work and the heat of the day' have the additional privilege of having spent a greater part of their lives in serving the King and have been able to enjoy the privileges of the Kingdom longer than those who come to faith in Jesus later in life. They should rejoice that others have come to the same inheritance because of the Lord's gracious and merciful generosity, not be full of negative grumbling.

Those who live as Kingdom children should submit to God's purposes rather than grumble against His mercy and righteousness. None received more nor less than what was promised them.

Anyone coming to a personal knowledge of Jesus and into the revelation of His Kingdom regrets what seem to be the wasted years before that great life-transforming event. The Lord promises to redeem 'the years the locust has eaten', and all who are part of the Kingdom, young or old, can serve the purposes of the King. He certainly rejoices over every sinner who repents and causes all heaven to rejoice with Him.

The cost of serving the King will be greater for some than others. 'From everyone who has been given much, much will be demanded; and from the one who has been entrusted with much, much more will be asked.' (Luke 12: 48)

Some 'have renounced marriage because of the Kingdom of heaven', (Matt. 19: 12) although that is not God's calling for every Christian. Some are told to sell everything they have, because their worldly riches stand in the way of their submission to God and dependence on Him. But that is not a universal law for all believers.

God does not ask for legalistic obedience, but for obedience which flows from a sincere love for the King and a desire to be faithful to His Kingdom purposes. It is not a matter of good intentions, but of actually doing His will.

THE TWO SONS

Jesus told another parable to illustrate this point. A man had two sons. He told the first to go and work in his vineyard and received the answer, 'I will not.' But 'later he changed his mind and went.' (Matt. 21: 29)

The father then told his second son to go and work in the vineyard. 'He answered, "I will, sir," but he did not go.' (v. 30)

Jesus simply asked the question: 'Which of the two did what his father wanted?' His listeners had no difficulty in answering correctly.

This is a telling little illustration. It is easy to be full of good intentions, saying what we should to the Lord, without our hearts being in what we are saying.

Time and again God's Kingdom purposes are going to conflict with our own plans and desires. Then our initial reactions tend to be like that of the second son; but if our hearts truly belong to the Lord, it is not long before we have repented of our selfishness, thought better of disobeying our Lord, and have done what He asked of us.

Jesus used this parable in a powerful way to warn the religious leaders and those who opposed Him. 'I tell you the truth, the tax collectors and the prostitutes are entering the Kingdom of God ahead of you. For John came to you to show you the way of righteousness, and you did not believe him, but the tax collectors and the prostitutes did. And even after you saw this, you did not repent and believe him.' (v. 31–2)

Religious pedigree will not ensure any person a place in the Kingdom; faith in Jesus will. Human goodness cannot earn such an inheritance; it does not matter how many and great a man's sins, God's forgiveness following repentance washes them all away. The way of self-righteousness is no substitute for true righteousness which can only be given through Jesus.

The life-style of the swindling tax collectors and immoral prostitutes demonstrated their rejection of the Kingdom, until such time as they repented and received that glorious inheritance. The religious are full of the right-sounding phrases and responses, but without actually repenting, submitting their lives to the heavenly King's authority. Those who repent, regardless of the nature of their former life, enter the Kingdom ahead of those who refuse to repent.

THE WEDDING BANQUET

Jesus told the parable of the Wedding Banquet to illustrate the fact that many who hear the gospel of the Kingdom refuse to respond. He said that the Kingdom of heaven is like a king who prepared a wedding banquet for his son. His servants carried the invitations to the guests, but they refused to come. He sent more servants to urge them to come as everything was prepared for them. 'But they paid no attention and went off – one to his field, another to his business. The rest seized his servants, ill-treated them and killed them.' (Matt. 22: 5–6) The king sent his army to destroy the murderers and to burn their city.

He was determined to have the banquet filled with guests.

So he told his servants: 'Go to the street corners and invite to the banquet anyone you find.' (v. 9) They did as they were told and found both good and bad. The banquet was filled; but those originally invited did not deserve the feast.

When the king came in to see the guests, one had no wedding clothes. 'How did you get in here without wedding clothes?' the king asked him. The man was speechless.

'Tie him hand and foot, and throw him outside, into the darkness, where there will be weeping and gnashing of teeth.' (v. 13) The parable concludes with the truth that 'many are invited, but few are chosen.' (v. 14)

Again it is impossible to avoid the obvious conclusion that many who had heard the gospel of the Kingdom would be passed over because they had never responded, and so had not been able to bear the fruit of the Kingdom in their lives. Hearing it again and again is no virtue if there is no heart response. Agreeing with the gospel is not the same as submitting one's life to the authority of the King.

Many are invited but few chosen, and those who are will have wedding garments. They will be clothed with the righteousness of Jesus so they can stand before their heavenly Father without fear of rejection or condemnation. They do not come in their own name, but in the name of Jesus who is the Way, and who shed His blood to make them acceptable in God's sight and able to inherit His eternal Kingdom.

He is not content with bringing the gospel of the Kingdom to those who are nominally His people; He sends His disciples out to all who will hear and respond. There can be no such person as a 'nominal Christian'. He is no Christian at all who is not part of the Kingdom of heaven. And all who are His children are sent out to witness, regardless of the rejection they suffer from those who oppose the gospel.

The Pharisees were always looking for an occasion to trap Jesus by what He said, much as those who fail to respond to the gospel today try to find some intellectual flaw in the argument of the Scriptures to excuse their unbelief. Even to

Nicodemus, who was an honest enquirer, Jesus said: 'I have spoken to you of earthly things and you do not believe; how then will you believe if I speak of heavenly things?' (John 3: 12)

MODERN 'PHARISEES'

There is no excuse for unbelief: 'Woe to you, teachers of the law and Pharisees, you hypocrites! You shut the kingdom of heaven in men's faces. You yourselves do not enter, nor will you let those enter who are trying to.' (Matt. 23: 13) Tragically even this Scripture has its parallel today.

Many who have been brought up in religious formalism in the churches are hungry for spiritual reality. They want to know the Lord and to experience His power in their lives. Increasingly, they hear of the movement of the Holy Spirit that is gathering momentum in this generation. However, many are held back by their clergy or leaders, for whom the Kingdom may not be a reality. They scoff at the idea of conversion, dismissing genuine experiences of God as 'mere emotionalism'. They claim there is no need to seek Him personally, only to be true to the traditions of the denominational church. To be faithful has been reduced, for some, to the level of attending a service weekly.

Such men are deeply offended at the suggestion that people need to repent and to submit their lives personally to the Lordship of Jesus. It is widely assumed that He is a God of universal love and everyone will be received into the Kingdom of God finally anyway.

This is not only to be deceived, but to lead others into deception.

Even when some of their people have genuine new birth experiences and know the power of the Holy Spirit in their lives, they are told that such things are of no consequence: 'You will soon get over it!' Often they are deliberately prevented from sharing their new-found faith with others in the congregation.

When they ask for instruction in the Scriptures, they are met with embarrassment. When they want to have a prayer meeting, permission is refused. They are reduced to frustration by the lack of leadership given to them.

Is it not true today of some: 'You yourselves do not enter, nor will you let them enter who are trying to'? How this must grieve Jesus.

Do those who scorn new birth experiences and the empowering of the Holy Spirit manifest the life and power of the Kingdom themselves? Is their preaching accompanied by signs following? Do they give the example of faith to their congregations? Are they men consumed with zeal to reach the lost with the good news of the Kingdom? Or are they men afraid to face their spiritual inadequacy, too proud to repent and cry out to God for His enabling?

TRANSFORMED MINISTRIES

Praise God that many clergy in recent years have experienced great changes in their ministries because they have sought God and met with Him. 'He who seeks finds; and to him who knocks, the door will be opened.' (Matt. 7: 8) I have lost count of the number of men, ordained for many years, who have testified to becoming Christians only recently. Their ministries have been transformed as a result. Instead of teaching religious observance and urging their congregations into church activity, they have been able to lead people into the Kingdom, see them filled with the Holy Spirit and have been able to encourage their growth in ministry. They have become teachers of the Word instead of critics of it, and have known dimensions of true praise and worship formerly beyond their experience.

The Church is not the Kingdom; neither is the Kingdom the Church. However a congregation of church people are properly those who are children of the Kingdom because all have come to true repentance and faith in Jesus. They share together the life of the Kingdom, pray together with the authority of the Kingdom and reach out into the world with the truth and power of the Kingdom. They are a people with a sense of mission and with zeal for God's purposes. Their personal devotion for Jesus is seen not only in their worship, but in their relationships also. They love one another and count the unity the Holy Spirit creates among them as precious.

When a church is a Kingdom-conscious people, Jesus causes it to grow both in depth and size. He tells His people to proclaim the Kingdom in word and deed and promises that He will build the Church.

Chapter 10

EACH ONE PRECIOUS

THE SHEEP AND COINS

Jesus told several parables expressing His desire to reach the lost with the good news of the Kingdom. If someone owning a hundred sheep loses one, what does he do? 'Does he not leave the ninety-nine in the open country and go after the lost sheep until he finds it?' (Luke 15:4) Having found it, he is so full of joy he gathers his friends and neighbours saying: 'Rejoice with me; I have found my lost sheep.' (v. 6)

What lessons does Jesus draw from this? 'I tell you that in the same way there is more rejoicing in heaven over one sinner who repents than over ninety-nine righteous persons who do not need to repent.' (v. 7)

Heaven rejoices with the Lord in seeing His reign extended, in seeing a lost soul under condemnation coming to repentance, new life and the inheritance of the Kingdom.

Jesus tells another similar parable of a woman with ten coins who loses one. She searches diligently and finds it. She too gathers her friends and neighbours to share her joy that what was lost has been found. 'In the same way, I tell you, there is rejoicing in the presence of the angels of God over one sinner who repents.' (Luke 15: 10)

How precious each soul is to the Lord! They are so precious that He sent His Son to die and thus save them from condemnation, death and hell. How it must grieve Him to see people turn away from Him and deny Him.

THE LOVING FATHER

The parable of the Loving Father (often known as the Prodigal Son, or the Two Sons) must be one of the best-known and most commonly quoted passages of teaching from the New Testament.

A man had two sons. The younger asked his father for his share of the inheritance, which he squandered on wild living in a distant country. When he had spent everything, there was a severe famine. In great need, he was hired to feed pigs and longed to eat their food; 'but no-one gave him anything.'

The son 'came to his senses' and decided to return home. His father saw him coming and ran to meet him, throwing his arms around him and kissing him. 'Father,' the son said, 'I have sinned against heaven and against you. I am no longer worthy to be called your son.' (Luke 15: 21)

The father ordered his servants to put the best robe on him, a ring on his finger and sandals on his feet. The fattened calf was to be killed so they could have a feast in celebration: 'For this son of mine was dead and is alive again; he was lost and is found.'

The older brother was angry when he came home from the fields to discover the feast was in honour of his brother. He refused to go in. His father came out and pleaded with him; but he only complained that he had never been given a feast to celebrate with his friends even though he had remained diligent and obedient – unlike his wasteful younger brother.

'My son,' the father said, 'you are always with me, and everything I have is yours. But we had to celebrate and be glad, because this brother of yours was dead and is alive again; he was lost and is found.' (vv. 31–2)

What a wealth of meaning is woven into each of Jesus's parables!

First we need to notice that both those brothers were sons of the father and therefore had an inheritance to come from him. When the younger son asked for his inheritance his father gave it to him, although he must have realised it would be wasted. There are many who ask for Kingdom inheritance, but because their lives are not truly submitted to the authority of God and they do not have genuine love for Him, they squander that inheritance. They are more intent on doing what they please and the Father knows He cannot force their love for Him.

However, He is always ready to extend His mercy and grace, His love and forgiveness to any who return to Him in repentance. Once that breaking and humbling has taken place, the son is able to enter into his father's joy. He experiences the father lavishing gifts on him that he certainly does not deserve. There is even a feast to celebrate his home-coming. The father is overjoyed that his son returned. Now he can allow himself to be loved by his father in a way he would not allow before.

The sin of the elder son was two-fold. First, he refused to forgive his brother, even though the father had forgiven him. But secondly he too had failed to live in the power of his inheritance. In that sense he was as bad as his brother.

'You are always with me,' the father tells the elder son, 'and everything I have is yours.' There are many today who have Kingdom inheritance and Kingdom resources available to them. But they are so busy, diligently serving with their human resources, they fail to take account of the divine, supernatural resources that are theirs through Jesus.

The parable teaches the folly of failing to live in the power of the Kingdom, and both brothers were guilty of that. Above all we see the amazing love and wisdom of the father in watching his younger son leave, knowing that he would have to wait until, willingly and humbly, he was prepared to accept his love.

What a picture of our heavenly Father's patience, refusing to force any of His children into love or obedience! Respecting their freedom of choice, He waits for their willing response to submit to His reign and rejoices in them when they do. He not only waits for the sinner, He pleads with the self-righteous to enter the joy of true inheritance.

THE SHREWD MANAGER

There was a rich man whose manager was accused of wasting his possessions. He was called to account and told he was dismissed.

At first the manager was perplexed as to what to do. He decided to summon his master's creditors and enquired how much each owed. The manager asked for immediate payment, but reduced the amounts due. His master commended him for acting so shrewdly. 'For the people of this world are more shrewd in dealing with their own kind than are the people of the light.' (Luke 16: 8)

Jesus then tells His listeners to 'use worldly wealth to gain friends for yourselves, so when it is gone, you will be welcomed into eternal dwellings.' (v. 9) This suggestion does not need to cause us problems; worldly wealth is to be used with wisdom and astuteness. There is no point in hoarding it, or 'storing it up in barns'. We certainly cannot take it into eternity with us. All financial resources and worldly wealth are given us to use.

Such generosity as the shrewd manager showed would seem out of place in the world's business standards and yet accomplishes far more than the cut-throat tactics of many traders. Jesus points out: 'Whoever can be trusted with very little can also be trusted with much, and whoever is dishonest with very little will also be dishonest with much. So if you have not been trustworthy in handling worldly wealth, who will trust you with true riches? And if you have not been trustworthy with someone else's property, who will give you property of your own?' (vv. 10–12)

A person's attitude towards money reveals so much about their spiritual attitudes. Do not store up for yourselves treasure on earth, Jesus said, 'But store up for yourselves treasures in heaven, where moth and rust do not destroy, and where thieves do not break in and steal.' (Matt. 6: 20) It is the rich resources of the Kingdom that have permanent value.

God knows our hearts. 'For where your treasure is, there your heart will be also.' (Matt. 6: 21) If a person lives for worldly wealth and advancement, that is where his heart is set – on things that pass away. If his heart is set on heavenly things, he has an eternal Kingdom as his inheritance and he will handle wisely, honestly and well the worldly resources put at his disposal.

'No servant can serve two masters. Either he will hate the one and love the other, or he will be devoted to the one and despise the other. You cannot serve both God and Money.' (Luke 16: 13) Whatever you serve becomes your master!

The Pharisees, who loved money, sneered at this teaching of Jesus. To them He said: 'You are the ones who justify yourselves in the eyes of men, but God knows your hearts. What is highly valued among men is detestable in God's sight.' (Luke 16: 15)

Jesus has received considerable criticism for commending the shrewdness of the manager. His purpose is to direct us to the things that truly matter. We are not created to serve money; money is there to serve us. As the children of the Kingdom we can afford to be generous, to forgive debts altogether, and God sometimes requires us to do that. 'But love your enemies, do good to them, and lend to them without expecting to get anything back.' (Luke 6: 35)

Such attitudes do not belong to the world; but they are of the Kingdom. Jesus continues: 'Then your reward will be great, and you will be sons of the Most High, because he is kind to the ungrateful and wicked. Be merciful, just as your Father is merciful.' (vv. 35–6)

THE RICH AND THE POOR

Jesus told the parable of the rich man and Lazarus. The one lived in luxury, the other was a beggar at his gate. Both died.

The beggar was carried by the angels 'to Abraham's side.' The rich man went to hell where he was tormented and cried out: 'Father Abraham, have pity on me and send Lazarus to dip the tip of his finger in water and cool my tongue, because I am in agony in this fire.' (Luke 16: 24)

Abraham replied: 'Son, remember that in your lifetime you received your good things, while Lazarus received bad things, but now he is comforted here and you are in agony. And besides all this, between us and you a great chasm has been fixed, so that those who want to go from here to you cannot, nor can anyone cross over from there to us.' (vv. 25–6) Our eternal destiny is determined by our actions in this life!

The rich man asked for someone to be sent to warn his brothers, who were no doubt also wealthy, disobedient unbelievers. He wanted them to be spared the torment he was experiencing. But he was told they had Moses and the Prophets to warn them.

The rich man persisted. Surely if someone from the dead went to them, they would repent! Jesus knew such an argument to be false: 'If they do not listen to Moses and the Prophets, they will not be convinced even if someone rises from the dead.' (Luke 16: 31)·

Sadly, this has proved prophetically true. Even though Jesus conquered death and rose again, the fact of His resurrection does not convince all. Faith comes from hearing the Word of God. Salvation comes from responding to that Word. Then a man believes whole-heartedly in the resurrection, because he has experienced the risen Christ for himself.

If we are living as the children of the Kingdom we know that all our worldly wealth is under the sovereignty of Jesus. He is ruler even in our financial affairs. Our substance is made available to Him for the extension of His Kingdom. Even with our money we put the Kingdom first.

Like so much of what Jesus says, this parable makes it abundantly clear that a man's eternal destiny is determined by his response to the gospel of the Kingdom during his life on earth. If he chooses to go his own way instead of following Jesus, he will discover he is lost for eternity. A great gulf will separate him from God and His glory. To reject the way of glory now will result in being excluded from it beyond death.

The wonder is that God makes His eternal glory available to sinners who are prepared to come to the cross in repentance and faith. He is willing to cancel all the sins, fears and doubts that have separated him from God and make all the riches of His Kingdom available to him.

THE KINGDOM WITHIN YOU

Jesus said: 'The kingdom of God does not come visibly, nor will people say, "Here it is," ' . . . because the kingdom of God is within you.' (Luke 17: 20–1) The Greek word translated 'within' can also mean 'among'. Although 'within' is the better rendering, both are true: the Kingdom is both within and among. It is not a visible Kingdom, a piece of territory; it is present wherever Jesus reigns in His sovereign power. It is present within those who live the life of the Kingdom, albeit imperfectly. God has planted the seed of the Kingdom within them, with all its potential. They are to demonstrate its presence, its power and reality in the world.

Wherever the King is, there the Kingdom is present. He is among those who gather in His name. So whenever Christians gather for fellowship or worship, the resources of the King and His Kingdom are present and available to them.

This means that worship should be dynamic. A conventional service, predictable in its lifelessness, is hardly an expression of Kingdom worship! The book of Revelation gives us a pictorial glimpse into the courts of heaven. There the heavenly host worship the Lord, continually aware that He reigns as the Holy King in majesty and glory.

Those who worship Him on earth are given access to His heavenly throne by Jesus: 'Therefore, brothers, since we have confidence to enter the Most Holy Place by the blood of Jesus, by a new and living way opened for us through the curtain, that is, his body, and since we have a great priest over the house of God, let us draw near to God with a sincere heart in full assurance of faith, having our hearts sprinkled to cleanse us from a guilty conscience and having our bodies washed with pure water.' (Heb. 10: 19–22)

The way into the holy Presence of the Lord is open to Christians. They can enjoy that privilege in this life and can be assured of enjoying that heavenly Kingdom eternally. Those who, like the rich man, fail to come to that living way and walk with Jesus, will find themselves separated from Him eternally – and will be unable to warn their loved ones of the dire consequences of their unbelief and disobedience. Those who recognise their need of forgiveness and salvation will come to Him and will discover His love, forgiveness and acceptance now, and the eternal reward of rejoicing with Him.

What a choice! And what does the cost of discipleship matter when so much is at stake? 'I tell you the truth,' Jesus said to them, 'no-one who has left home or wife or brothers or parents or children for the sake of the kingdom of God will fail to receive many times as much in this age and, in the age to come, eternal life.' (Luke 18: 29–30)

Chapter 11

FREE TO BE POSITIVE

SET FREE

'It is for freedom that Christ has set us free,' says Paul. (Gal. 5: 1) It is always important to notice the tenses of the verbs used in Scripture. Here the apostle points his readers to the fact of what God has already done for them in Christ: they *have been* set free.

Free from what? Free from bondage to the law, from trying to please God and win His favour through obedience to a code of legalistic practice, knowing that they will inevitably fail to do so. Free from relating to God by religious observance instead of through a loving personal relationship in which He is known as 'Father'.

Free from bondage to the flesh, so that human passions and desires no longer rule them. Their minds, wills and emotions can be brought under the sovereignty of the Holy Spirit. It is no longer the law of sin and death that operates within them, but the law of the Spirit of life.

Free from the devil's dominion. They have been rescued by Jesus from the dominion of darkness and brought into the Kingdom of God. Satan no longer need have any control over them. The only activity he is allowed in their lives is that which they willingly choose to give him through their disobedience.

Free from the demands of worldliness. They no longer have to live as the world lives, no longer conformed to the pattern of this world, but transformed through the renewing of their minds. Their values have been completely changed by their seeking first the Kingdom and allowing Jesus to reign over their lives.

All this is accomplished because of what Jesus did on the cross. There sin was dealt with, the power of negative bondage was broken. There sinners were crucified with Christ, so that they may be dead to the old life lived without Him and alive with new life lived in Him.

The believer is freed from the power of the negative kingdom and is given the gift of the positive Kingdom.

Paul contrasts these two for the Galatians. 'The sinful nature desires what is contrary to the Spirit, and the Spirit what is contrary to the sinful nature. They are in conflict with each other, so that you do not do what you want.' (Gal. 5: 17)

The sinful nature is negative by nature, which is why we live in such a negative world. It is therefore utterly opposed to the working of God's Spirit, who is positive by nature. 'The acts of the sinful nature are obvious:' says Paul, 'sexual immorality, impurity and debauchery; idolatry and witchcraft; hatred, discord, jealousy, fits of rage, selfish ambition, dissensions, factions and envy; drunkenness, orgies, and the like.' (Gal. 5: 19–21) Such things are obviously not the working of God's Spirit. As far as He is concerned, they are all negative and stand opposed to His positive Kingdom.

So Paul warns: 'I warn you, as I did before, that those who live like this will not inherit the kingdom of God.' (Gal. 5: 21) How can anyone inherit the Kingdom when he lives a life opposed to the very nature of this spiritual Kingdom? That is like suggesting a man should be honoured by one nation, while being a traitor who has spied for another.

God is not to be mocked and will not be fooled. It is not those who call Him 'Lord' who will be part of that Kingdom, but those who do His will.

When a man accepts the power of the cross in his life, he is freed from all the sin and bondage of the past. He does not have to look back or imagine that he is held back by spectres of his past. Faith in the atoning work of Jesus sets him free from the past. He is now a new creation with a new heart.

Jesus said: 'Every good tree bears good fruit, but a bad tree bears bad fruit. A good tree cannot bear bad fruit.' (Matt. 7: 17–18) Then he warns: 'Every tree that does not bear good fruit is cut down and thrown into the fire.' (v. 19) It is good for nothing else.

CALLED TO BE FRUITFUL

At the Last Supper, He made it clear that God expects fruitfulness in the lives of His children because He wants to be glorified in their lives: 'This is to my Father's glory, that you bear much fruit, showing yourselves to be my disciples.' (John 15: 8)

Fruitfulness can only be through the activity of the Holy Spirit within the believer. So, having warned the Galatians of the negative things of darkness that prevent a person from inheriting the Kingdom of God, he then goes on to speak of the fruit of the Spirit.

'But the fruit of the Spirit is love, joy, peace, patience, kindness, goodness, faithfulness, gentleness and self-control.' (Gal. 5: 22–3) All these are definitely positive by nature and in their effect on the believer and those around him. They are in striking contrast to the negative works of the flesh.

The Christian may want more of the positive fruit of the Spirit in his life, but he is often painfully aware of the pull towards the negative things of the flesh. All too often he has to confess he has sinned by doing the very thing that stands opposed to the working of God's Kingdom in his life.

Does this mean he stands condemned before God, or is not truly a part of His Kingdom, or stands in danger of losing his inheritance?

He cannot be in condemnation if he knows God's forgiveness, which blots out his transgressions as if they never happened. The page is wiped clean and He does not keep on record the sins that have been forgiven. There is no condemnation for those who are in Christ Jesus. How could there be condemnation in the Son of God or in His Kingdom? The believer has been brought out of the kingdom of darkness, where all are under condemnation, and has been brought into the Kingdom of light, where there is no condemnation.

The Lord has planted the seed of the positive Kingdom in a life that has been conditioned to be negative. Although the cross has dealt with all those negatives, the individual Christian has to learn how to apply the victory of the cross to the circumstances of his life so that he may live in freedom. He has to allow the water of the Holy Spirit to nurture that seed towards maturity and greater fruitfulness in his life.

A LIFE OF CHOICES

The fact that he still thinks, reacts and behaves in negative ways should not be surprising. *He no longer needs to do so* and the Lord will continue to teach him not to do so. God's refining in his life will result in change so that he chooses increasingly to live Kingdom life, rather than react or indulge himself in a fleshly way. As he matures in the life of the Spirit, he will choose to live according to his rich Kingdom inheritance, rather than choose the alternative of fleshly disobedience.

Of course if a man chooses to walk his own way, deliberately denying his inheritance, then the life of the positive Kingdom will be choked, as Jesus makes clear in the parable of the Sower.

Although Kingdom life can only be lived through the grace and power of the Holy Spirit within the believer, God does require his co-operation with the Spirit. He will never interfere with the Christian's free-will, for He desires a loving response to His purposes.

STAND FIRM

Paul gives sensible, practical advice to his readers: 'Stand firm, then, and do not let yourselves be burdened again by a yoke of slavery.' (Gal. 5: 1) Stand firm against all the pressures to live negatively. Stand firm against the temptations to allow your faith to be reduced again to the level of religious observance. Stand firm against the devil tempting you to indulge yourself and express the old nature; stand firm against him and he will flee from you. Stand firm against the pressures of worldliness and the desires to be accepted by those who live worldly lives, by allowing your standards to be reduced to theirs. Stand firm against the desires you know to be alien to God's purposes for you. Stand firm against the temptation to contradict God's Word, to believe you know better than the truth He reveals. Stand firm against the desire to compromise His Word in your life. Stand firm against the temptation to neglect what is necessary for your spiritual health and what the flesh dislikes: prayer, study of the Scriptures, praise and worship, sharing your faith with others. How the flesh dislikes such things!

'The only thing that counts is faith expressing itself through love.' (v. 6) To live by faith is to depend on what God has accomplished already for you through Christ. You will walk in liberty as you trust in the victory He has already won over all the negative forces of evil. You do not have to fight a battle He has already fought and won; you only have to trust in His victory. Fighting the good fight of faith is applying that victory to the circumstances of your life.

The positive Kingdom of God can only be manifested when people live by faith, faith that is expressed in love. For this is a Kingdom of both faith and love. In no way are these two contradictory; they are complementary.

Faith is a way of life; it cannot suddenly be switched on in a time of need. Love is another aspect of the same way of life. It is to be expressed by the Christian at all times in all situations, not only when he chooses to do so.

'A little yeast works through the whole batch of dough,'
Paul warns. (v. 9) Satan encourages Christians to be negative.
The mind is his first line of attack. He feeds to the believer a
negative thought that will stimulate fleshly desire, or a doubt
that will undermine faith, or an unloving thought that will
inspire criticism, judgment, fear or even hatred. If the first
negative is received he is quick to follow it with another and
then another. It is not long before the Christian finds himself
in a totally negative frame of mind, at which point he is easy
prey for the enemy to begin accusing him. He will suggest
that his fleshly desires demonstrate how unacceptable he is to
God; his doubts are an indication of how weak and feeble his
faith is; his critical, judgmental attitudes show how unlike
Jesus he is and totally unworthy of His Kingdom.

If the negative thoughts and the accusations are believed,
the Christian feels utterly condemned. But if he had stood
firm against the first negative the whole process could not
have developed.

Satan is the father of all lies; he is to be resisted. He wants to
sow seeds of negativity within us so that we do not act
positively with faith and love as the children of the Kingdom
of God.

'A little yeast works through the whole batch of dough.'
One negative can easily lead to a completely negative,
unbelieving attitude. But in the same way, the seed of the
positive Kingdom can cause positive life to flow through the
believer. As Satan sows the negative seed from without, so the
Holy Spirit sows the positive seed from within.

He is the voice of God within you, and constantly draws
you to God's words and gives you the witness as to what is,
and is not, right in His sight. To believe the word He speaks is
to encourage faith; to act on that word is always to act in love.

Negative attitudes and actions have a repercussive effect on
others around. One person expressing negative criticism can
easily affect others, so that they too become critical. They may
have no knowledge of the particular matter, but if they receive

the criticism the spirit of criticism will influence them to pass on judgmental attitudes to others.

Many ungodly situations arise among Christians (as well as others) in this way. There can even be pleasure in criticising others – the result of pride and a lack of self-assurance.

Similarly, Christians can, and should be, an influence in spreading the attitudes of the positive Kingdom. In this way they are to be leaven in the lump, light for the world and the salt of the earth. Their difficulty is to spread the positive in the midst of so much negativity. They will be ineffective in doing this unless they stand firm against the temptation to be negative in their own lives.

Our mouths so often give us away. Jesus says it is from the overflow of the heart that the mouth speaks. If we say negative, unbelieving, critical things, that is only an indication of what is going on in our hearts. The new heart given at new birth becomes tainted by sin and needs to be purified. We need to ask God, not only to forgive the negative things that persist in our experience, but to purify our hearts. With David each of us can pray: 'Create in me a pure heart, O God, and renew a steadfast spirit within me.' (Ps. 51: 10)

Again and again we shall have to reckon ourselves dead to sin. We do not need to live in it any longer. If you imagine that you are still in bondage to it, you will simply resign yourself to a life of constant spiritual failure, which is totally the opposite to the Kingdom life God intends for you. Jesus does not reign in failure! 'You, my brothers, were called to be free.' (Gal. 5: 13) So live in the glorious liberty of the sons of God. You do not have to live as if still a child of the devil, resigned to serving him. You do not have to give him any pleasure or satisfaction by responding to his temptations to make you negative again.

Even when you do, for none of us is without sin, you do not have to give him further satisfaction by allowing him to accuse you. He cannot accuse you in heaven; he has been expelled. You, however, are a child of the Kingdom and reign in Christ Jesus. The Lord sees you sitting in heavenly places where Satan does not belong. You do not have to allow him to kick you around like a spiritual football. You have the power to stand firm against him and see him flee, and the authority to dismiss him from the circumstances of your life in the name of Jesus.

He always seems to know where to attack as he probes for our weaknesses. We give him a foothold in our lives by our love of sin and desire to please ourselves, rather than our heavenly Father. When we set our hearts on living in righteousness we resist the enemy and find that he is ineffective in luring us with temptations that previously seemed too alluring to resist.

LIBERTY, NOT LICENCE

As Christians, we are free from the bondage to law. We can serve God by following the leading of the Holy Spirit. But Paul warns of a subtle temptation: 'Do not use your freedom to indulge the sinful nature.' (Gal. 5: 13)

Freedom in Christ is not freedom to do what we like. It is being free to love Him and therefore to love others. And so Paul continues in the same verse: 'rather, serve one another in love. The entire law is summed up in a single command, "Love your neighbour as yourself." If you keep on biting and devouring each other, watch out or you will be destroyed by each other.' (Gal. 5: 13–15)

It is freedom to walk away from the negative and live in the positive power of God. To sin deliberately is an act of rebellion against God, and He does not reign in rebellion. We deny our position as Kingdom children by such actions. That undermines the power of God in our lives, and prevents Him from working through us in the way He desires.

The secret is not to have our hearts and minds set on ourselves and our own desires, but on Him and our wish to please Him. 'So I say, live by the Spirit, and you will not gratify the desires of the sinful nature.' (Gal. 5: 16)

The best way to counteract the negative is to concentrate on the positive, to seek first the Kingdom and to fix your eyes on the King: 'Therefore, holy brothers, who share in the heavenly calling, fix your thoughts on Jesus, the apostle and high priest whom we confess.' (Heb. 3: 1)

Concentrate on the negative and you will become pre-occupied with it, and will spend your Christian life fighting all the ungodly desires you have. Concentrate on Jesus and you concentrate on the positive King who has overcome the negative. Draw near to Him and come near to the One who is altogether positive.

Speak as He speaks, and you speak positively. Think with the mind of Christ, and you think positively. Act in obedience to the leading of His Spirit, and you act positively. 'Since we live by the Spirit, let us keep in step with the Spirit.' (Gal. 5: 25)

For the Christian life is a walk with Jesus. It is not a static life, holding on to what you hold dear, resisting change, doubting your prayers will be answered. It is moving on with Jesus in the way He leads, taking His positive life into the negative world. Where there is doubt, we can bring faith. Where there is bitterness and resentment, we can bring forgiveness. Where there is sorrow, we can bring joy. Where there is hopelessness and despair, we can bring God's hope. Where there is sickness, we can bring His healing. Where there is bondage to evil spirits, we can bring deliverance in the name of Jesus. Where there is need, we can bring the Lord's provision. Where there is fear and anxiety, we can speak the words of His peace. Where there is futility, we can bring His purpose. Where there is weakness, we can bring His power and strength.

Wherever there is the negative we can bring the power of His positive Kingdom to bear. We are commissioned by Him personally to do just that. And wherever the positive meets the negative the positive prevails, as when light meets darkness the light prevails.

There has to be a constant determination to think, speak

and act according to the principles of the positive Kingdom to which you belong. There needs to be an equally constant determination to resist every impulse to think, speak and act negatively – the way of the world, the flesh and the devil. In both, the Holy Spirit will be your helper if you are prepared to call on Him.

Chapter 12

RIGHTEOUSNESS, PEACE AND JOY

'The kingdom of God is not a matter of eating and drinking, but of righteousness, peace and joy in the Holy Spirit, because anyone who serves Christ in this way is pleasing to God and approved by men.' (Rom. 14: 17–18)

Paul is referring to religious rules about food and drink. No observance of religious rules will enable a person to enter the Kingdom, or empower him to live as a child of the Kingdom. It is only by the working of the Spirit within him that the Christian can express the life of the Kingdom in righteousness, peace and joy. Only by the Spirit is he able to please God and to live the godly life approved by men.

To live as a child of the Kingdom is to live in righteousness, in right standing with God, in right relationship with Him, walking with Him in righteous ways. The Spirit will cleanse and purge out of your life all that is unrighteous. He will convict you of the sin of deceit and untruthfulness, whether in your personal relationships or business practices. He will convict you of unbelief and your failure to trust the Lord. He will teach you to believe His promises and expect His positive answers to prayer. He will show you where you fail to love and are filled instead with self-love, selfishness and self-pity.

To live as a child of the Kingdom is to know that you are at peace with God because, having been convicted, you have repented and turned away from your sins. You have been forgiven because of the grace, mercy and love of your heavenly Father. You know you are forgiven and that nothing interferes with your unity with God; you have received peace beyond understanding and have a sense of total well-being before God.

Furthermore, this peace leads to joy. As a child of the Kingdom, you know that no man or situation can steal your joy from you. No one can snatch you from the hand of your heavenly Father, whom you delight to serve. Everything is working together for good because of your love for God, and because you are called according to His purpose. Even in the midst of adversity you rejoice in Him. You learn that you are able to rejoice in the Lord always, for at no time are you deprived of Him or of the treasure of His Kingdom.

THE FRUIT OF RIGHTEOUSNESS

Because the Kingdom is a matter of righteousness, peace and joy in the Holy Spirit, we should expect to see the power of the Kingdom evidenced in miracles and signs of His Kingly power and authority among us. Paul certainly did. In fact, he did not consider that he had fully preached the gospel of the Kingdom unless he could demonstrate its presence with works of power: 'I will not venture to speak of anything except what Christ has accomplished through me in leading the Gentiles to obey God by what I have said and done – by the power of signs and miracles, through the power of the Spirit. So from Jerusalem all the way around to Illyricum, I have fully proclaimed the gospel of Christ.' (Rom. 15: 18–19)

These words should encourage all preachers of the gospel. Whenever and wherever that same gospel of the Kingdom is proclaimed today, in the power of the same Holy Spirit, the signs and miracles can be seen. God is as powerful today as ever, His words as efficacious and His Spirit as freely given. Only unbelief in the preacher or people can hinder the demonstrations of Kingdom power. 'Our gospel came to you not simply with words, but also with power, with the Holy Spirit and with deep conviction.' (1 Thess. 1: 5)

Certainly the power and evidence of the Kingdom will not be seen where there is unrighteousness. 'Do you not know that the wicked will not inherit the kingdom of God? Do not be deceived: Neither the sexually immoral nor idolaters nor adulterers nor male prostitutes nor homosexual offenders nor thieves nor the greedy nor drunkards nor slanderers nor swindlers will inherit the kingdom of God.' (1 Cor. 6: 9–10)

It is not unknown to have people from some, or all, of these categories claming to be Christians, while persisting in their sinful ways. Paul continues: 'But you were washed, you were sanctified, you were justified in the name of the Lord Jesus Christ and by the Spirit of our God.' (v. 11)

The Christian is expected to manifest a transformed life, because he is intent on living as a child of the Kingdom rather than persisting in his old ways.

If we have new life, we are to live new lives. If we are to inherit the Kingdom, we are to live Kingdom lives. We are cleansed from the old, made acceptable to God and filled with His Spirit to make this possible. It is He 'who has qualified you to share in the inheritance of the saints in the kingdom of light.' (Col. 1: 12) So why continue to walk in darkness?

Paul is confident: 'The Lord will rescue me from every evil attack and will bring me safely to his heavenly kingdom.' (2 Tim. 4: 18) All those who seek first the Kingdom of God in their lives can dare to have a similar confidence.

Of His Son, God says: 'Your throne, O God, will last for ever and ever, and righteousness will be the sceptre of your kingdom. You have loved righteousness and hated wickedness; therefore God, your God, has set you above your companions by anointing you with the oil of joy.' (Heb. 1:8–9) He desires all His children to love righteousness, and it is only by living in light that Christians will be able to bring effectively the gospel of light into the darkness of the world.

Our God is the consuming fire, who purges and cleanses

the lives of believers and who stands in judgment on all unrighteousness.

James asks: 'Has not God chosen those who are poor in the eyes of the world to be rich in faith and to inherit the kingdom he promised those who love him?' (James 2: 5) Like Paul, he emphasises the twin pillars of faith and love. The children of the Kingdom will be men and women of faith and love. They are to be rich in faith. God delights to see His children laying hold of eternal life, applying the victory of the cross to their circumstances and availing themselves of the heavenly resources at their disposal. They are not to be negative, denying their inheritance, saying they are weak in faith, without blessing or resources. Faith enables them to enter more and more fully into all that is already theirs in Christ.

Our love for the Lord is always the motivation for obedience to His purposes. Disobedience points to a crisis of love.

Peter bids us make our calling and election sure by making every effort to add to our faith goodness, knowledge, self-control, perseverance, godliness, brotherly kindness and love. These things will keep us from being ineffective and unproductive. Without these qualities Christians are 'near-sighted and blind' and have forgotten the significance of being cleansed from past sins.

With these qualities believers will never fall and 'will receive a rich welcome into the eternal kingdom of our Lord and Saviour Jesus Christ.' (2 Peter 1: 11)

God requires your performance to be the evidence of your position before Him. It is no use claiming to have relationship with Jesus, if your life does not demonstrate evidence of that; or saying that you are a child of the Kingdom if you do not live accordingly. He knows we do not become perfect in our performance overnight; but He does expect progress and perseverance so that with John you can say: 'To him who loves us and has freed us from our sins by his blood, and has made us to be a kingdom and priests to serve his God and Father –

to him be glory and power for ever and ever! Amen.' (Rev. 1: 5–6)

Chapter 13

KINGDOM FAITH

Jesus devoted Himself to prayer during His earthly ministry.
If it wasn't possible to be alone with His Father because of the
pressures of ministry and the demands of the people, He
prayed through the night. Nothing must stand in the way of
maintaining fellowship with His Father in prayer.

'Then Jesus told his disciples a parable to show them that
they should always pray and not give up.' (Luke 18: 1) In this
story there was a judge 'who neither feared God nor cared
about men.' (v. 2) A widow kept coming to him pleading for
justice against her adversary. Although for some time he
refused, he finally gave her justice to stop her from
persistently bothering him.

'And will not God bring about justice for his chosen ones,
who cry out to him day and night? Will he keep putting them
off? I tell you, he will see that they get justice, and quickly.
However, when the Son of Man comes, will he find faith on
the earth?' (vv. 7–8)

Jesus does not separate prayer from faith. The woman
believed in her cause and so was prepared to be persistent.
Jesus says His chosen ones are prepared to call out to Him day
and night and will receive justice *quickly*.

Often Christians pray in a tentative and half-hearted
manner, as if hardly daring to believe their heavenly Father
would answer their cause. There is little virtue in prayer itself;
Jesus warns that we shall not be heard for our many words.
But prayer that is a true expression of positive faith will

receive positive answers from God. The promises Jesus gives us overwhelmingly point to this truth. 'I will do whatever you ask in my name, so that the Son may bring glory to the Father. You may ask me for anything in my name, and I will do it.' (John 14: 13–14)

The all-embracing nature of this promise seems startling and almost unbelievable, especially to those who have prayed, but with little consideration of the faith God looks for in our praying.

To pray in the name of Jesus is to pray in the person of Jesus, to pray as He would. He always prayed with faith, with the expectation that He would receive from His loving Father what He asked for. It is inconceivable to think that He would have prayed without faith, for all that is not of faith is sin; and Jesus certainly never sinned.

To pray with faith, so that God answers our prayers, will bring glory to the Father and is the evidence of fruitful Kingdom living. 'You did not choose me, but I chose you to go and bear fruit – fruit that will last. Then the Father will give you whatever you ask in my name.' (John 15: 16) Again the promise is both emphatic and far-reaching: 'whatever you ask'. 'I tell you the truth, my Father will give you whatever you ask in my name.' (John 16: 23)

If we allow Him, the Holy Spirit will guide us in our praying. We are to pray at all times 'in the Spirit'. He will not only show us what to pray but will inspire the faith with which to pray.

FAITH OR HOPE?

Sometimes we have to acknowledge that we lack the faith necessary for a situation. As an extension of our Kingdom Faith ministry, God impressed on the elders of the Bethany Fellowship the need to open a college where people could be trained for ministries that would be effective in the life and power of the Kingdom.

Within a few days we heard of a college in the near vicinity that was for sale. When we viewed this, it was ideal for our needs. When we prayed, it seemed right to offer £570,000 plus £10,000 for the contents – in cash. We are a faith ministry looking to the Lord for His provision. We do not raise money, nor do we ask others for it. If we have need, we pray to our Father in heaven.

We did not have the money when making the offer, but we were confident that this was the property God was wanting us to use for the college. Later we heard that our offer was accepted (although there had been higher ones) because we were the only ones to be offering cash! You need to be sure of your guidance from God before taking such a step of faith.

This happened just prior to my departure to the Far East for a time of ministry. While there I had to face a personal dilemma. Although I had often been in similar positions of faith, never had the sum involved been so great. I had to face the fact that I was not in a position of faith for nearly £600,000.

I believed God wanted us to have the college and I knew that He *could* supply the money. But that is not faith. I believed that He *would* supply the money; but that is not faith either. It is hope to believe that something will happen in the future. Faith says it has already happened, even if you have no visible evidence to substantiate your confidence.

When Jesus taught His disciples to pray with faith, He told them: 'Therefore I tell you, whatever you ask for in prayer, believe that you have received it, and it will be yours.' (Mark 11: 24)

Believe that you have received it. I believed my heavenly Father could supply the necessary money, that He would do so; but I did not believe I had received it.

When you are not in a position of faith you can either shrug your shoulders and say that this cannot be the will of God, or you can seek Him for the faith you need. The former course is actually unbelief. I had to begin my seeking by confessing my unbelief and asking for God's forgiveness.

He usually uses our times of seeking Him to sort out several issues in our lives, and I experienced a prolonged time of repentance lasting about two hours. This was followed by a timely encounter with the Lord in which I also received healing from Him. The details are unimportant for our purposes here.

He then said to me: 'Colin, I give you a million dollars.' Now faith comes from hearing God. Immediately I knew God had given the faith I needed. I was up from my knees and dancing around my hotel room with joy, praising God for His generosity.

I could not see the money, but it was as if it had already dropped on to the bed. I could go back to England and tell the others in the fellowship, 'The Lord has given me a million dollars.' That encouraged others in their faith. In Scripture, leaders are to give an example of faith for others to follow.

In the following months the Lord supplied about £280,000, but that was barely half way to the amount needed. There was only one week to go before the money was due to be paid when I left for an extensive time of ministry in Australia. There had been moments of doubt since my encounter with the Lord; but I had always had to repent of them and praise the Lord for the million dollars.

On the day before the money was due I telephoned home, but was told the money had not arrived. However, everyone was at peace, confident the Lord had the whole matter in hand. I also was given peace by the Lord, although I felt a tremendous sense of responsibility. It seemed we had laid our whole ministry on the line.

The other elders had to tell the vendors we did not have all the money, but were praying for it! They did not share our faith in prayer, but we had good relationships with them during the negotiations over the property, and they offered to delay completion for a further month. That had to be the final dead-line.

Every time I 'phoned home I was told that no further gifts of a substantial nature had been received. On my way to England from Australia I stopped for twenty-four hours in the city where I had received the promise from God of the million dollars. I was due to speak at two services there.

Some friends had invited my companions and me to dinner before driving us to the airport. At the end of the meal, my friend asked me how the college project was going. I said we were really on the faith rack, needing £300,000 by the following Friday. To my astonishment he said that his bank would wire the money to our bank so that we would have the money in time to complete the purchase.

Three hundred thousand pounds is one million dollars of the currency of that nation!

On the plane I discovered that a Jumbo jet is not the ideal place to dance in the Spirit! It was not the money itself that was the cause of joy. Being given such a sum seemed unreal, and I never saw the money. It simply passed from one bank to another. It was the faithfulness of God that was overwhelming. He had spoken, He had promised and He had provided.

Needless to say, I was deeply grateful also for my friend who had been the loving, responsive channel of His giving. The purchase was duly completed and the college was full for its first term, without any need to advertise for students!

Hope says it will happen; faith believes it has! 'If you believe, you will receive whatever you ask for in prayer,' says Jesus. (Matt. 21: 22)

AGREEING TOGETHER

The power of agreeing together in faith is immense. During the whole episode of the college, my great friend and fellow-elder Bob Gordon was at the heart of things. He is now director of the college and was utterly convinced of God's purpose in supplying the money. When others questioned whether our guidance was right, or doubted that the Lord would provide, Bob would direct them to both the written word of Scripture and the many spoken words of prophecy God had given us.

It encouraged him no end when I returned from the Far East with the promise God had spoken to my heart, and there were several times when we were reminded of the Scripture: 'Again, I tell you that if two of you on earth agree about anything you ask for, it will be done for you by my Father in heaven. For where two or three come together in my name, there am I with them.' (Matt. 18: 19–20)

Again we are faced with the tremendous resources God makes available to those who agree in faith. God is always willing to supply whatever resources are necessary for the work of His Kingdom. James points out that some do not receive because they do not have the faith even to ask: 'You do not have, because you do not ask God.' (James 4: 2) And he also warns about asking out of wrong, selfish motives. 'When you ask, you do not receive, because you ask with wrong motives, that you may spend what you get on your pleasures.' (James 4: 3)

CONFIDENCE BEFORE GOD

John, like James, heard Jesus make all His prayer promises. Writing his first Epistle some fifty years later, he could look back over a long time of ministry and see that the promises held good: 'Dear friends, if our hearts do not condemn us, we have confidence before God and receive from him anything we ask, because we obey his commands and do what pleases him.' (1 John 3: 21–2)

We do receive anything we ask from God, but we need confidence before Him. That confidence comes out of knowing you are in a right relationship with Him, cleansed of your sins by the blood of Jesus and that you are listening to His Word. Furthermore that word needs to be obeyed because your heart desire is to please Him. In other words, these prayer promises are set within the context of living in the power of the Kingdom.

We ask in the name of Jesus as we seek to follow Him, our lives submitted to His authority. Just as effective prayer cannot be separated from faith, so it cannot be separated from the lives we live. Prayer cannot be seen as an activity separated from the rest of life. We pray as the people we are, out of the relationship with God that we have.

'This is the assurance we have in approaching God: that if we ask anything according to his will, he hears us. And if we know that he hears us – whatever we ask – we know that we have what we asked of him.' (1 John 5: 14–15)

Here again in John's words is that same confidence and the all-embracing scope of the word 'whatever'. If we pray in the name of Jesus, we pray in the will of God, led and inspired by His Spirit. He has given us His Spirit to water the seed of the Kingdom planted within us as believers in Jesus Christ. Part of the fruit that is borne out of that seed is the confidence to ask in prayer, believing it is God's purpose to give us whatever we ask in Jesus's name. 'Ask and it will be given to you... For everyone who asks receives... how much more will your Father in heaven give good gifts to those who ask him!' (Matt. 7: 7, 8, 11)

God does not want you to feel condemned because of what appears to you as previous failure in prayer. If you think that in some situations you have been guilty of praying without faith, then confess that sin immediately and know the forgiveness of God. Do not allow the enemy to have any victory over you.

Often groups of Christians have prayed for a sick person and believed confidently that God would heal him. Their faith is shattered if the person dies. 'We really felt God was going to heal him,' they will say.

It is not always easy to point out lovingly that faith does not say God will do something, but believes He already has done it. Even if a promise is given, it has to be appropriated with that same mustard-seed faith. It is such a tiny thing but makes all the difference. It brings about the transformation needed in the situation.

In prayer we are to come with confidence, but not pride. Jesus told the parable of the Pharisee and the tax collector to illustrate this: 'To some who were confident of their own righteousness and looked down on everybody else, Jesus told this parable'. (Luke 18: 9) Two men, a Pharisee and a tax collector, went to the Temple to pray. The Pharisee prayed about himself: 'God, I thank you that I am not like all other men – robbers, evildoers, adulterers – or even like this tax collector. I fast twice a week and give a tenth of all I get.' (v. 11–12)

The tax collector would not even look up to heaven but beat his breast and said: 'God, have mercy on me, a sinner.' (v. 13) Jesus said that he went home justified, acceptable in God's sight, not the Pharisee. 'For everyone who exalts himself will be humbled, and he who humbles himself will be exalted.' (v. 14)

If that is what Jesus says, it will surely happen. What God requires of us more than anything else is that we come humbly and honestly before Him, prepared to confess our sins and whatever unbelief is in our hearts. There is no point in trying to make God think we believe and trust Him when we don't. He is willing to give us faith when we admit our need of it.

In my hotel room in the Far East two hours of heart-searching under the convicting power of the Holy Spirit, a time of further breaking in my life, preceded the word of faith I needed to receive from the Lord. May He forgive us for all the perfunctory and superficial prayers we pray. And may He draw us before His throne of grace, humble in the knowledge of what we are in ourselves, yet overwhelmingly grateful for His forgiveness and love. May He speak words of faith to our hearts as we wait on Him, for He is the rewarder of those who diligently seek Him.

Chapter 14

KINGDOM POWER AND AUTHORITY

In the life of every Christian there are moments of crisis or decision which will have far-reaching impact on his life. The events at Caesarea Philippi were particularly significant for Jesus's disciples.

They had heard His teaching about the Kingdom, including many of the parables. They could see the Kingdom as a present reality, not only by the things Jesus said, but also by what He did. The Kingdom had not come theoretically; it had come in power. 'Jesus went through all the towns and villages, teaching in their synagogues, preaching the good news of the kingdom and healing every disease and sickness.' (Matt. 9: 35)

The presence of the Kingdom was manifested in the way Jesus ministered to the needs of the people. He brought the positive power of God to bear on their negative situations. Nothing could be more negative than to be in spiritual bondage to Satan.

DEMONS ROUTED

Many today who do not have experience of ministering in the power of the Kingdom doubt the existence of demons. In some cultures their presence is more obvious than others, as they are openly worshipped and invoked by prayer or to bring curses on others. But the occult is present everywhere with all its demonic activity. People consult spiritualists and mediums, ignorant perhaps of the direct commands of Scripture not to do so; many certainly ignorant that they consult demonic forces, not the living God.

Others are involved in freemasonry and other societies, whose beliefs are contrary to the gospel of the Kingdom (even though Scriptures may be read at their meetings) and whose practices are demonically inspired.

The devil certainly does not want people to believe in demons. He is the deceiver who encourages the things of secretive darkness. The children of light have nothing to hide. It is folly for anybody to close his eyes to the nature of what he is involved in, because of personal gain and influence or because he enjoys the camaraderie.

Jesus certainly believed in demons, evil spirits that are messengers or servants of the devil. They could possess people causing them great torment (as with 'Legion', the man possessed by many demons); they could cause sickness and disease, and they could oppress people spiritually.

Some try to explain away these manifestations of evil spirits by saying that Jesus used the thought-forms and beliefs of His time. This will not do. It is heresy to suggest that Jesus, the Truth, should lie or deceive the people by supporting beliefs He knew to be untrue. That is completely contradictory to His purpose and ministry. He corrects error and falsehood, and teaches His disciples to do the same. He was in constant confrontation with the Pharisees because of their hypocrisy: they said one thing and inwardly believed something totally different. It is unthinkable that Jesus could be open to the same charge.

He knew the reality of the demonic spirits, and the gospel accounts are full of references to His power and authority over these. This is hardly surprising. We have noted already how Satan and the angels who followed him in rebellion were immediately thrown out of heaven. Jesus is the King of heaven and wherever His sovereign power is brought to bear those demonic forces have to give way to His authority.

'People brought to him all who were ill with various diseases, those suffering severe pain, the demon-possessed, the epileptics and the paralytics, and he healed them.' (Matt. 4: 24) Those with need were attracted to Jesus because they saw He had the power and resources to meet those needs, including the ability to free them from demonic forces. 'When evening came, many who were demon-possessed were brought to him, and he drove out the spirits with a word and healed all the sick.' (Matt. 8: 16)

The way Jesus dealt with demons was by ordering them out of people's lives with authoritative commands; 'he drove out the spirits with a word'. For example, to Legion He said: 'Come out of this man, you evil spirit!'

Demons could talk through the one they possessed, although nowhere does Jesus become involved in lengthy conversations with them. In fact He would not let them speak because they knew His identity. On this occasion, He gave permission for the evil spirits to enter two thousand pigs who immediately 'rushed down the steep bank into the lake and were drowned.' (Mark 5: 13)

This may seem to be a senseless waste; but Jesus was allowing a demonstration of the destructive power and intention of these demonic forces.

A demon-possessed man who could not talk was brought to Jesus. 'And when the demon was driven out, the man who had been dumb spoke. The crowd was amazed and said, "Nothing like this has ever been seen in Israel." ' (Matt. 9: 33)

'Then they brought him a demon-possessed man who was blind and dumb, and Jesus healed him, so that he could both talk and see. All the people were astonished and said, "Could this be the Son of David?" ' (Matt. 12: 22–3)

His power over demons not only amazed the people, but encouraged this searching question as to whether He was their long-expected Messiah, their King from heaven. The Pharisees accused Him of casting the demons out by

Beelzebub, the prince of demons. They could not face the implications of this being the hand of God at work.

Jesus made it clear that this was indeed the work of God and the very evidence that, with His coming, the Kingdom had come. 'But if I drive out demons by the Spirit of God, then the kingdom of God has come upon you.' (Matt. 12: 28)

He made it clear to those who opposed Him: 'I tell you the truth, the Son can do nothing by himself; he can do only what he sees his Father doing, because whatever the Father does the Son also does.' (John 5: 19) Jesus came to perform the works of His Father. When we see the Son at work, we see the Father at work. He desires to see His people free from demonic bondage and from sickness; and He sends His Son to demonstrate that the power of His Kingdom is greater than all the powers of darkness.

The demonic causes of sickness are not always evident. The other disciples were unable to heal the epileptic boy while Jesus was on the Mount of Transfiguration with Peter, James and John. When they descended, Jesus upbraided them for their unbelief. Then 'Jesus rebuked the demon, and it came out of the boy, and he was healed from that moment.' (Matt. 17: 18)

This is not to suggest that all sickness is due to demon-possession. There are numerous occasions when Jesus healed people without there being any references to demons. Certainly all sickness is negative and cannot be a manifestation of the positive Kingdom of God.

The Lord, however, is able to redeem every evil situation. He can use negative experiences to bring people through to a closer walk with Himself, or to a true appreciation of the power and reality of His Kingdom. This is not to imply that sickness is His best purpose for His children. He allows the negative to bring us to deeper repentance, to sharpen our faith and trust in Him.

Matthew certainly sees both deliverance from evil spirits and healing of every infirmity and disease by Jesus as a fulfilment of Isaiah's prophecy: 'He took up our infirmities and carried our diseases.' (Isa. 53: 4 – quoted in Matt. 8: 17) They were evidence that He was the Messiah, the Man sent from heaven with the message and gift of the Kingdom. They were signs that accompanied the proclamation of the gospel.

THE CRUCIAL QUESTION

The dialogue between Jesus and His disciples at Caesarea Philippi was a crunch point because it was then that Jesus said to them: 'But what about you? Who do you say I am?'

In the light of the evidence of all they had heard Him say and seen Him do, who did they think He was? No doubt for some time this question had occupied much of their thinking and discussion. None of them had dared to speak out that He was the Messiah, even if they had thought Him to be. To Jews such a suggestion, if untrue, was blasphemous.

On this occasion however, Peter blurts out the glorious revelation: 'You are the Christ, the Son of the living God.' (Matt. 16: 16) Jesus immediately commends him, telling him he has received revelation from His heavenly Father. He then speaks of the building of His Church which hell cannot overcome and says: 'I will give you the keys of the kingdom of heaven; whatever you bind on earth will be bound in heaven, and whatever you loose on earth will be loosed in heaven.' (Matt. 16: 19)

The precise translation of the original Greek is important here. The translation above suggests that if something is bound by Peter it will then be bound in heaven, or if loosed by him it will be loosed in heaven. Jesus actually told Peter that what he binds on earth is *already* bound in heaven; what he looses on earth is *already* loosed in heaven.

The apostle binds on earth what is already bound in heaven; he is given the authority to do that because by proclaiming Jesus to be the Christ, the Messiah, the King sent from heaven, he receives the authority of the Kingdom.

Similarly, he is given authority to loose what is loosed in heaven.

That same authority is given to all who submit their lives to the authority of Jesus and so become part of His Kingdom. They do not need to allow any of the powers of darkness to bind them or keep them in oppressive bondage.

Jesus sends His disciples out with the Kingdom authority to speak the words of the Kingdom and to perform its acts of power. As soon as Peter proclaims Jesus to be the Christ, He warns them that He must be rejected and killed, although on the third day He will be raised to life.

This same Peter immediately wants to argue: 'Never, Lord!' he said, 'This shall never happen to you.'

Earlier he was the mouthpiece of the heavenly Father; now he speaks for the enemy! 'Jesus turned and said to Peter, "Out of my sight, Satan! You are a stumbling block to me; you do not have in mind the things of God, but the things of men."' (Matt. 16: 23)

Jesus directs the rebuke to Satan. He constantly tries to direct people away from God's purposes and encourages them to view every situation rationally, with the limited perspective of human understanding. Revelation expands the mind rather than diminishing our thinking capacity.

The revelation that He is King expands the thinking of the disciples towards Jesus. Satan immediately tries to counteract that. But Jesus is alert to his devices. He uses His Kingdom authority to dismiss Satan from the situation. He will go forward in the way the Father sets before Him and will allow nothing to divert Him from that.

MOVING ON WITH JESUS

And then He points out to His disciples the cost of following Him. They are to exercise Kingdom authority and power in their lives. If they do, they will have to face opposition and cost: 'If anyone would come after me, he must deny himself and take up his cross and follow me. For whoever wants to save his life will lose it, but whoever loses his life for me will find it.' (Matt. 16: 24–5)

No man will be able to serve his own ends and those of the Kingdom at the same time. No man will be able to submit his life to Jesus as King and still reign himself, ruling his own life with stubborn independence. Acknowledging the kingship and lordship of Jesus means that the 'self' in his life has to be dethroned.

The greater the submission to the authority of Jesus in his life, the greater the authority of Jesus can be exercised in a Christian's life. The Lord gives Kingdom authority to every believer; his capacity to exercise that authority is determined by his submission to God's authority in his life.

Peter would have to learn to submit to His plans and purposes, not argue with the Lord, if he was to exercise properly the Kingdom authority Jesus was giving him.

Jesus goes on to speak of His return in glory with His angels, when the full authority of His sovereignty will be established on earth. Each man will then receive his due reward, and Jesus adds: 'I tell you the truth, some who are standing here will not taste death before they see the Son of Man coming in his kingdom.' (Matt. 16: 28)

This does not imply that Jesus thought His Second Coming would take place during the disciples' lifetimes. Elsewhere He makes it clear that the Father alone knows the timing of that event. However, it does imply that some of those disciples, like Peter, were going to experience the reality, the authority and power of His Kingdom. Mighty things are to happen to him and through him in others' lives.

Later Jesus addresses these same words to the disciples generally: 'I tell you the truth, whatever you bind on earth will be bound in heaven, and whatever you loose on earth will be loosed in heaven.' (Matt. 18: 18) Again we are faced with the tremendous authority and power available to the children of the Kingdom, a power that is to be manifested also in prayer. Christians are called to live in Christ's victorious power.

Jesus does not separate prayer from faith. All the prayer promises He gives presuppose that we pray in faith expecting the answer we need from God. He does not anticipate receiving the answer 'No'! So in the very next verse, after telling the disciples of their Kingdom authority to bind and loose, He says: 'Again, I tell you that if two of you on earth agree about anything you ask for, it will be done for you by my Father in heaven.' (Matt. 18: 19)

This is not agreement in a form of words, but agreement in faith, being in full accord and harmony. Such unity is a basic principle of Kingdom living. The promises Jesus gives show the tremendous resources available to the children of the Kingdom.

Nothing will upset the flow of authority and power in Christians' lives quicker than pride and its consequent disunity. On one occasion the disciples argued among themselves as to who was the greatest – while walking along with the Son of God! On another occasion they asked who was the greatest in the Kingdom of heaven.

Jesus answered by standing a child in their midst and saying: 'I tell you the truth, unless you change and become like little children, you will never enter the kingdom of heaven. Therefore, whoever humbles himself like this child is the greatest in the kingdom of heaven.' (Matt. 18: 3–4) The principles of God's Kingdom are the opposite of worldliness. Jesus Himself came as the humble servant and yet was the Man of authority and power.

As we have seen, a man has to humble himself under the authority of Jesus if he is to enter the Kingdom; he needs to stay in a place of humble submission to Him if he is to exercise Kingdom authority and power effectively. The proud cannot enter the Kingdom, and authority will not be given to those who want to exalt themselves rather than Jesus. Simon the sorcerer offered Peter and John money, hoping to buy the ability to lay hands on others to receive the Holy Spirit. He was rebuked strongly, told to repent and get his heart right before God.

To His Kingdom children God gives His commission. His gifts cannot be earned or bought; they are freely given to equip them for witness and ministry. Jesus made so much spiritual power available to the disciples; and yet faith and obedience had to be exercised or they would not be able to avail themselves of the authority at their disposal. Put very simply, because they were children of the Kingdom Jesus was teaching them a simple truth: whatever I can do you also can do.

We can sympathise with the disciples in finding it difficult to grasp such a truth, for the same principle holds good to this day. The Lord wants to see His authority and power exercised in the lives of believers, so they can proclaim and demonstrate that the Kingdom of God is among us *today*!

Chapter 15

SENT OUT

It was not long before Jesus sent His disciples to share the message of the Kingdom and demonstrate its power: 'As you go, preach this message: "The kingdom of heaven is near." Heal the sick, raise the dead, cleanse those who have leprosy, drive out demons. Freely you have received, freely give.' (Matt. 10: 7-8)

Jesus's own proclamation had been that the Kingdom was near; so this was to be their message. Whatever He had said, they were to say. He had healed the sick, so they too were to heal. He had cast out demons in their presence; now they were to take authority over them and cast them out in His name. They were even to raise the dead!

No doubt they found it easier to identify with His words; 'I am sending you out like sheep among wolves.' But He also promised that when they were under pressure and persecution they need not worry what to say; 'At that time you will be given what to say, for it will not be you speaking, but the Spirit of your Father speaking through you.' (vv. 19-20)

This is an important principle of ministry. It is not God's purpose that we should work for Him, but that He should work through us. Only then will we be able to do the things He does: 'I tell you the truth, anyone who has faith in me will do what I have been doing. He will do even greater things than these, because I am going to the Father.' (John 14: 12)

When He returned to the Father, He prayed for the Holy Spirit to be given. Only by His Spirit working in us can we speak from God and work signs and wonders in His name.

It was not only to the original twelve that Jesus gave such commands, with the expectation they would use their Kingdom faith and authority to execute them. He sent out seventy-two other disciples with a similar charge; and when He gave His great commission to the Church in His risen body, He said: 'All authority in heaven and on earth has been given to me. Therefore go and make disciples of all nations, baptizing them in the name of the Father and of the Son and of the Holy Spirit...' (Matt. 28: 18–19)

That much is commonly quoted, but the sentence continues: '*and teaching them to obey everything I have commanded you.*' (v. 20) As the nations came to faith in Jesus, they too would see the same authority and power being manifested in Jesus Himself as in the lives of those first Christians.

'*Anyone who has faith*', Jesus says, '*will do what I have been doing.*' Such statements as this have always challenged the faith of Christians, both individually and corporately. It is much easier to opt for the notion that such power and authority was only for the apostolic age, although there is nothing in Scripture to warrant such a position. Quite the opposite. The life and power of the Kingdom have not diminished at all since the time of Jesus.

SIGNS FOLLOWING

Those first disciples saw the power of God at work as they went out to proclaim the gospel of the Kingdom. They did not go out as healers, miracle-workers or as those seeking signs as ends in themselves. They were sent out with the Kingdom message, but expected their words to be confirmed by God with demonstrations of Kingdom power. They expected to see signs following the preaching of the Word.

Signs will not accompany preaching that is only a pale imitation of the gospel, or a partial gospel that has selected certain moral or pastoral elements of what Jesus said. The gospel of the Kingdom embraces the whole counsel of God.

Signs are the evidence that Kingdom power and authority is still given to men. The first disciples did not manifest such gifts as perfectly as Jesus. Their perception, faith and authority fell far short of His. There was nothing imperfect in Jesus to hinder His unity with His Father. The works of heaven could be seen supremely in Him.

Nevertheless, the disciples did see God working powerfully through them. The seventy-two were overjoyed that 'even the demons submit to us in your name.' (Luke 10: 17)

The disciples were sent out in Jesus's name and all the works they performed were in His name – on His behalf, with His power and authority.

Similarly today, believers are not only to speak in His name but work in His name, on His behalf, with His power and authority. Anyone who has faith in Jesus will do what He did – and even greater things still.

IN THE POWER OF THE SPIRIT

The fulfilment of this promise began on the day of Pentecost. The Holy Spirit came on the disciples gathered in Jerusalem. When they preached the gospel, three thousand became Christians and the Spirit came upon them also. Nothing like that had happened during the earthly ministry of Jesus, because the Spirit had not then been poured out.

Once they were filled with the Spirit, those diffident men became men of power and authority. Instead of God being with them in His Son, He was now in them by His Spirit. This was the greater event that would cause their joy to be full, as Jesus had promised at the Last Supper.

With the coming of the Spirit, the disciples had received the power Jesus promised when appearing to them in His risen body. The opening chapter of Acts tells us that, 'He appeared to them over a period of forty days and spoke about the kingdom of God.' (Acts 1: 3) He told them not to leave Jerusalem but to wait for 'the gift my Father promised'. (v. 4)

'In a few days you will be baptised with the Holy Spirit,' He said, (v. 5) and then explained the implications of that: 'You will receive power when the Holy Spirit comes on you; and you will be my witnesses in Jerusalem, and in all Judea and Samaria, and to the ends of the earth.' (v. 8)

After these promises had been fulfilled at Pentecost, the transformation in these men immediately became apparent. First they were filled with such praise for God, He needed to give them languages they had never learned to enable them to express the joy in their hearts. The crowd that gathered heard them declaring the wonders of God in these other languages.

During the days that followed many believers were added to their number. 'Every one was filled with awe, and many wonders and miraculous signs were done by the apostles.' (Acts 2: 43) Notable among these was the healing of the crippled beggar at the Temple gate.

They also proclaimed the gospel of the Kingdom with increased boldness. When arrested and brought before the Jewish Council, they were forbidden to speak in Jesus's name again. They counted it more important to obey God than men, and so returned to their preaching. But not before holding a prayer meeting.

The content of their prayer is significant. With the hardening of opposition, they realised their need to see God act more powerfully in their ministries. No longer were they the fearful men meeting secretly for fear of the Jews. Now they are men of the Spirit, given by God to water the seed of the Kingdom planted in them. So they pray: 'Enable your servants to speak your word with great boldness. Stretch out your hand to heal and perform miraculous signs and wonders through the name of your holy servant Jesus.' (Acts 4: 29–30)

They had been before the council for their boldness; they recognised their need for greater boldness. They had seen great healings, still they prayed for God to stretch out His hand to heal. They were moving in the dimension of the miraculous; they asked for more in the name of Jesus.

And how does God answer such prayer? 'After they prayed, the place where they were meeting was shaken. And they were all filled with the Holy Spirit and spoke the word of God boldly.' (Acts 4: 31) They had another Pentecost. God knew their need was to be filled with the Holy Spirit again. That was not to deny the value or validity of their former experience. They were learning that as Kingdom men with the commission to extend the Kingdom of God on earth, they were going to need constant empowering by the Holy Spirit.

Even though they did not ask for another infilling of the Holy Spirit on this occasion, God knew that to be their need. This was His answer to their prayer which expressed their heart-cry. And He shook the building to demonstrate that the wind of the Spirit was blowing on them afresh – why else do such a thing? He was not simply revitalising the gift within them; He was coming upon them in the person of the Holy Spirit with a fresh anointing.

If those first disciples were intent on preaching the gospel of the Kingdom, and seeing the signs and wonders that evidenced the presence of that Kingdom, they were also concerned to see that the church in Jerusalem established a corporate life consistent with the principles of the Kingdom: 'They devoted themselves to the apostles' teaching and to the fellowship, to the breaking of bread and to prayer.' (Acts 2: 42)

FELLOWSHIP

Kingdom people are men and women of the Word, with their lives deeply rooted in the gospel of the Kingdom. To have fellowship is to share life together. Those early believers were learning that to belong to God's Kingdom involves sharing your life with other Kingdom children. 'They broke bread in their homes and ate together with glad and sincere hearts.' (v. 46)

The all-embracing nature of their fellowship has been a

challenge to the Church ever since. 'All the believers were together and had everything in common.' (v. 44) 'No-one claimed that any of his possessions was his own, but they shared everything they had.' (Acts 4: 32)

Just as some have wanted to believe that the authority and power those early Christians enjoyed passed away with the apostolic age, so there have been those who say that such fellowship is an impossible ideal today. It is a temptation to reduce Scripture to the level of our experience, instead of seeing our experience raised to the level of Scripture.

There is nothing in the teaching of Jesus to support the idea that our commitment to Him and to one another is to be less today than in Biblical times, or that His power among believers will not be as great now as then. These are attractive ideas if we want to diminish the meaning and significance of Christian discipleship; but that is certainly not God's purpose.

Even in the history of the Church there have always been those who have experienced the signs and wonders (many are recognised as particular saints by some churches), just as there have been expressions of corporate fellowship similar to that described in Acts.

These cannot be imitations of the Biblical precedent. Both the signs and fellowship were the work of the Holy Spirit then and will be today, wherever He is allowed liberty in the lives of contemporary Christians.

Kingdom life and Kingdom power are inseparable. They are perfectly united in Jesus. As the early Christians lived the teaching He had given, so they saw God's powerful acts which demonstrated His Kingly presence among them.

Every expression of Kingdom life mirrors something of the nature of the King Himself. Forgiveness is a good example.

THE UNMERCIFUL SERVANT

Jesus told the parable of the Unmerciful Servant when Peter asked how often he was supposed to forgive his brother. The

Kingdom of heaven is like a king who wanted to settle accounts with his servants. A man who owed him millions was unable to pay; so the master ordered that he and his family be sold. The servant begged for patience and promised to repay the debt. The master took pity on him, cancelled the debt and ordered his release. Such is God's forgiveness for each of us!

The master was angry when he discovered that same man had demanded repayment of a paltry debt owed him by a fellow servant, only to have him thrown into prison when unable to pay. 'You wicked servant,' the master said. 'I cancelled all that debt of yours because you begged me to. Shouldn't you have had mercy on your fellow servant just as I had on you?' (Matt. 18: 32–3) In anger the master had him thrown in jail until he could pay back all he owed.

Jesus ends the parable by saying: 'This is how my heavenly Father will treat each of you unless you forgive your brother from your heart.' (v. 35)

In one parable Jesus embraces several principles of what it means to live as Christians, as children of His Kingdom. For example:

Blessed are the merciful, for they will be shown mercy. (Matt. 5: 7)
I tell you that anyone who is angry with his brother will be subject to judgment. (Matt. 5: 22)
Forgive us our debts, as we also have forgiven our debtors. (Matt. 6: 12)
For if you forgive men when they sin against you, your heavenly Father will also forgive you. But if you do not forgive men their sins, your Father will not forgive your sins. (Matt. 6: 14–15)
Do not judge, or you too will be judged. For in the same way you judge others, you will be judged, and with the measure you use, it will be measured to you. (Matt. 7: 1–2)
In everything, do to others what you would have them do to you. (Matt. 7: 12)

The Sermon on the Mount is about practical Kingdom living, about practical holiness which, in its simplest terms, is living like Jesus. This sermon is a moral ideal impossible to attain, unless those who seek to live it know they are children of the Kingdom with the life of God's Holy Spirit within them to enable them to do so.

In this particular parable Jesus makes it clear that to be an inheritor of the Kingdom is not sufficient; to have such a privilege involves the Christian in the responsibility of living Kingdom life, learning to react as Jesus would in each situation.

This will be demanding in many respects, for it is not possible for part of a believer to be in the Kingdom and another part outside. The Holy Spirit is watering the seed of the Kingdom placed within the believer so that the positive life of that Kingdom can replace all the negative areas. This is a process of sanctification, of making the believer holy in person and behaviour like Jesus. The more the Christian's life corresponds to that of the King, the more fruitful he will be as a witness of the Kingdom in the world. He will be more positive in faith, attitudes, thoughts and actions and less negative in his response to difficult situations.

If he is living as a child of the Kingdom, the Christian will bear witness by his actions as well as his attitudes, that he has been freed from the negative and is no longer in bondage to the world, the flesh and the devil. In Christ he has been set free!

Chapter 16

FACING THE COST

There is cost for those who would be true to Jesus, the cost of willingly and daily taking up a personal cross to follow Him: 'If anyone would come after me, he must deny himself and take up his cross and follow me. For whoever wants to save his life will lose it, but whoever loses his life for me will find it.' (Matt. 16: 24–5)

This cross does not represent what is imposed on the Christian against his will, like sickness or fear. It is what he willingly takes upon himself in order to be obedient and faithful to the King of kings. Nothing must come before Him, or the life and work of His Kingdom, in the order of his priorities. God and His Kingdom come first.

THE COST OF GIVING

Whatever is sacrificed for the Kingdom will be repaid many times over in this life, with the reward of eternal life as well! To take the gospel of the Kingdom into the world has always involved cost. It cost Jesus His human life. The disciples left their occupations and had to experience long periods of separation from their families to follow Him.

Physical comfort and worldly security often have to be sacrificed so that others can receive the good news of the Kingdom. It is costly to take needy people in your home in order to share Kingdom life with them. It is demanding to live for others rather than yourself. And yet those who love the King are devoted to the extension of His Kingdom, and are prepared to face the inconveniences that the demands of love often make and the sacrifices required to make Him known.

There is no greater joy than knowing the King and serving the cause of His Kingdom, seeing others receive the revelation that they are forgiven, made acceptable to God, have received the gift of the Kingdom, have been set free from their bondages and can love and worship the King in the beauty of His holiness. There is no greater joy than knowing you have fulfilled His command to feed the hungry and serve the needs of the destitute, both spiritually and physically:

> Is not this the kind of fasting I have chosen: to loose the chains of injustice and untie the cords of the yoke, to set the oppressed free and break every yoke? Is it not to share your food with the hungry and to provide the poor wanderer with shelter – when you see the naked, to clothe him, and not to turn away from your own flesh and blood? (Isa. 58: 6–7)

All this is costly to do in practice and yet it is rewarding, not only for the individual believer or for the recipients of his love, but for the whole cause of the Kingdom in the nation:

> Then your light will break forth like the dawn, and your healing will quickly appear; then your righteousness will go before you, and the glory of the Lord will be your rear guard. Then you will call, and the Lord will answer; you will cry for help, and he will say: Here am I. (Isa. 58: 8–9)

Obedience to the Lord releases His activity and provision into our lives. He literally multiplies back what is given to Him. Desire for more is not the motive behind the giving, but the desire to serve the King and express the life of His Kingdom. That involves expressing Him in the people we are, and therefore in the things we do:

> If you do away with the yoke of oppression, with the pointing finger and malicious talk, and if you spend yourselves on behalf of the hungry and satisfy the needs of the oppressed, then your light will rise in the darkness, and your night will become like the noonday. The Lord will guide you always; he will satisfy your needs in a sun-scorched land and will strengthen your frame. You will be like a well-watered garden, like a spring whose waters never fail. (Isa. 58: 9–11)

The measure you give is the measure you receive back! And yet there can be no comparison between the two. We give ourselves in our frail, human weakness and sinfulness; He gives Himself in His majesty and glory. We seek to serve the spiritually oppressed and hungry, taking to them the good news of the victory of Jesus and the freedom available through Him; and we receive the eternal gift of His Kingdom. We feed the physically poor and hungry, and He promises that we shall lack nothing ourselves.

The cost is in giving before you see the reward. Our willingness to give depends on how much self-love there is in us, whether we love ourselves more than Jesus and those He gives us to love. We need to be dead to that love of self. He said: 'I tell you the truth, unless an ear of wheat falls to the ground and dies, it remains only a single seed. But if it dies, it produces many seeds.' (John 12: 24)

Look how productive the death of Jesus has been. The Son of God gave His life that many sons might be drawn into the Kingdom. The principle is the same in our lives; 'the man who hates his life in this world will keep it for eternal life. Whoever serves me must follow me; and where I am, my servant also will be. My Father will honour the one who serves me.' (John 12: 25–6)

Jesus is emphatic: 'Anyone who does not carry his cross

and follow me cannot be my disciple.' (Luke 14: 27) So it is as well for those who want to serve the King to count the cost of doing so. He points out that if a man wants to build a tower he first calculates the cost of doing so. He will be ridiculed if he completes the foundations and then runs out of money. 'In the same way, any of you who does not give up everything he has cannot be my disciple.' (v. 33) Everything is available to the King and the work of His Kingdom.

The rich man wanted to enjoy his wealth in self-indulgence and was blind to the needs of the poor man at his gate. It is possible to close our eyes to the needs of those around us when the Lord has made material and spiritual things available to us to share with others. That is an essential part of Kingdom life: to share whatever we have with others. And it is Kingdom faith to believe that we shall not be the losers by doing so. We shall receive back what we have given many times over in this life, and in the age to come we shall rejoice eternally with our heavenly King.

PAUL'S CROSS
Paul's own testimony bears this out:

> As servants of God we commend ourselves in every way: in great endurance; in troubles, hardships and distresses; in beatings, imprisonments and riots; in hard work, sleepless nights and hunger; in purity, understanding, patience and kindness; in the Holy Spirit and in sincere love; in truthful speech and in the power of God; with weapons of righteousness in the right hand and in the left; through glory and dishonour, bad report and good report; genuine, yet regarded as imposters; known, yet regarded as unknown; dying, and yet we live on; beaten, and yet not killed; sorrowful, yet always rejoicing; poor, yet making many rich; having nothing, and yet possessing everything. (2 Cor. 6: 4–10)

This amazing testimony demonstrates how the positive power of God's Kingdom overcomes all the negatives. Throughout the history of the Church, other Christians have experienced similar trials with similar fortitude and victory. No matter how negatively the world treats those living in righteousness, their positive testimony wins through. The purity, understanding, patience, kindness and sincere love given by the Holy Spirit endures through all the troubles, hardships and distresses. The truthfulness and genuineness of those who remain faithful withstand all the lies and false accusations against them inspired by the enemy. Out of their poverty of spirit, many are made rich in the Lord. Nothing can take away their joy and their inheritance. Having nothing, they possess everything.

We have the treasure of the Kingdom in earthen vessels. The power of God can shine through our lives to give Him glory, and to demonstrate that He is the source of that power, and not us. And so Paul can say: 'We are hard pressed on every side, but not crushed; perplexed, but not in despair; persecuted, but not abandoned; struck down, but not destroyed.' (2 Cor. 4: 8–9)

Perseverance in the face of opposition was a feature of Paul's life. At Ephesus, for example, he spoke boldly in the synagogue for a period of three months 'arguing persuasively about the kingdom of God.' (Acts 19: 8) Some obstinately refused to believe and maligned his teaching before he left them. When he summoned the elders of the Ephesian Church while on his way to Jerusalem, he reviewed his time of ministry with them.

He preached the gospel of the Kingdom to them, he says, and in so doing did not hesitate to preach anything that would be helpful to them. No compromise for Paul in order to please the people! He did not hesitate 'to proclaim to you the whole will of God.' (Acts 20: 27) He did not pick and choose the attractive parts of the gospel at the expense of the more demanding things Jesus taught.

When he leaves them he commends them 'to God and to the word of his grace, which can build you up and give you an inheritance among all those who are sanctified.' (v. 32) It is only by facing the gospel in its entirety that they would be prepared for the inheritance that awaits those who are sanctified, made holy in God's sight through the cleansing blood of Jesus and the indwelling of the Holy Spirit.

DISCIPLINE

Perhaps there is no area where we try to excuse ourselves more than that of prayer. A Christian seeking first the Kingdom and God's righteousness will be a praying person. Yet we often excuse ourselves by delaying our prayer times or only praying in a superficial or cursory manner. We claim we are so busy or too tired.

Our God is a Lord of order and He wants to bring spiritual order, as well as physical, emotional, financial, political and social order into our lives. Spiritual order is rooted in discipline. We need a life of discipline if we are going to prevail in prayer, learning how to pray through to a victorious answer, setting our sights clearly on our objective and praying until that target is achieved.

Jesus anticipated that those who received the revelation that they were part of the Kingdom would give their lives to see the Kingdom extended. This would become their reason for living. To profess love and honour for the King without being concerned about the cause of His Kingdom, would be hypocrisy.

This was certainly the emphasis throughout the earthly ministry of Jesus and also in the life of the early Church. When Jesus appeared to His disciples in His risen body, it might have been anticipated that He would have taken the opportunity to teach them the principles of church planting, structure and organisation. But instead He continued to teach them about the Kingdom: 'He appeared to them over a period of forty days and spoke about the kingdom of God.' (Acts 1: 3)

The apostles followed their Lord's example. In Samaria Philip 'preached the good news of the kingdom of God and the name of Jesus Christ'. (Acts 8: 12) At Lystra, Iconium and Antioch, Barnabas and Paul warned: 'We must go through many hardships to enter the kingdom of God'. (Acts 14: 22) Here they refer to the full manifestation of the Kingdom that lies in the future. To live as Kingdom people now will involve obedience, sacrifice, persecution and hardships before the heavenly reward can be enjoyed. However, no disciple is ever without the Lord's presence or power, and the resources of heaven are available to him no matter what his situation or need.

Chapter 17

FOLLOWING JESUS

All those who are children of the Kingdom of God are called to be disciples of Jesus. A disciple is one who puts the claims of Jesus first in his life, regardless of the cost to himself. He lives, not to serve himself, but the King of Heaven. He enjoys the privileges of the Kingdom, but also faces the responsibilities that are his as a child of God.

Because Jesus Christ is his Lord, everything in his life is to be submitted to the authority of Jesus. The disciple is called to be holy, to be like Jesus. The more he submits to the Lordship of Jesus, the more Christ-like he becomes both in character and actions; and the more he is then able to enjoy his privileges.

'Whatever you do, whether in word or deed, do it all in the name of the Lord Jesus, giving thanks to God the Father through him.' (Col. 3: 17) The name in Scripture denotes the person. To speak and act in the name of Jesus is to speak and act in the person of Jesus: to say what He would say, or do what He would do in your position. That is made possible because God has given us His Kingdom life and has empowered us with the Holy Spirit. We have within us the same life that indwelt Jesus; and we have available to us the same Kingdom resources.

When Jesus called His disciples to follow Him, He wanted them to follow His example, both in life and ministry. They were to proclaim the Kingdom in word and power. And He was uncompromising in teaching what He expected of disciples.

Today many Christians have settled for a level of discipleship that bears little resemblance to the teaching and expectations of Jesus. Would He even recognise as true disciples many of those who claim to follow Him? His words are often compromised by believers either out of expediency, or to avoid personal cost.

As a result, many Christians fail to be the witnesses God wants them to be and, in many places, the Church is regarded as weak, ineffective or irrelevant.

God's children are to demonstrate the life-transforming presence of Jesus in the world. He calls them to face the implications of true discipleship, to be obedient and faithful to the Lord irrespective of personal cost to themselves. There are many privileges to being children of the Kingdom; there are also great responsibilities.

Out of love for Jesus, disciples are willing to apply His standards to their lives. A discipleship without cost is not true discipleship. Christians are called to deny themselves and take up their cross daily in order to follow Christ. That cross is not a burden imposed upon them, but what they willingly undertake for the sake of the gospel.

God comes first in their lives, before consideration of self; His will matters above all else. To put God first before either personal considerations, or even loved ones, is best both for the disciple and all those he loves.

It is one thing knowing what we ought to do; it is another thing actually to do it. How can we apply the principles of the Kingdom to our lives so that we might live in the good of them?

We can ask ourselves the question: What would Jesus do in my position? How would He think? What would His attitude be if placed in similar circumstances? What would He believe and how would He pray about a particular matter? What does Jesus want of me at this moment? If He was standing by me, what would I do? Would I be ashamed of doing some things I do normally, if I was so aware of His presence?

In most situations the disciple would be able to answer such questions easily, through his knowledge of Scripture and by listening to the witness of the Holy Spirit. There may be some occasions when he would be genuinely perplexed. That would encourage him to seek the Lord for clear guidance; he would not want to step outside God's purposes.

Even when he perceives what Jesus would do, he will still be tempted to disobey if obedience would prove costly. That would be to place love of self above love for the Lord. Jesus said that those who love Him obey Him.

The Christian is not going to face up to the demands of true discipleship unless he sets his heart on doing so. He will need to make a firm decision that he is going to walk as Jesus did. This is God's calling on his life and there is no lesser calling for any Christian. John says: 'Whoever claims to live in him must walk as Jesus did.' (1 John 2: 6) This is a must for all Christians. When a person becomes a Christian he is placed in Christ and he is to live accordingly. Jesus Himself said: 'Whoever serves me must follow me; and where I am, my servant also will be. My Father will honour the one who serves me.' (John 12: 26)

The flesh does not like obedience or cost. It is futile to settle for a level of discipleship acceptable to us, and imagine that it will be acceptable to God. Our decision to follow Jesus is not an emotional response to the gospel, but a definite act of the will. There is little point in making decisions that are not implemented.

THE VITAL QUESTION

In every situation ask yourself the question, WHAT WOULD JESUS DO? – and then do it! Your life will come more into line with what He desires of you. Don't be put off by the expectation of failure. God can use your failures positively to show you when you do not want to obey Him, or fail to trust Him.

You must decide for yourself what the Christ-like action would be in any particular situation. Even if you pray with others, or talk over a certain matter with them, the ultimate decision is yours. That is your responsibility as a disciple of Jesus. You need to decide what you believe in conscience Jesus would do in your position, and then do it!

You are not making decisions about anyone else's conduct, only your own. You have no right to judge others for the decisions they make.

There will be occasions when you need to submit significant decisions to those who are in spiritual authority over you. You need not fear to do that, if you genuinely want the will of God for your life. Disciples do not act in independence; they are, however, to be personally responsible for their actions.

You need to agree to apply this principle to every area of your life, otherwise you will avoid the question when you want to avoid cost. You agree to do what Jesus would do regardless of the cost to yourself, even if this involves loss of position or prestige in the eyes of the world. Financial loss could result if you are compromising your Christian principles by being involved in dubious business practices. Better to walk with Jesus in righteousness than to walk with the ungodly.

There will be times when you fail to follow Jesus; but these will be because of errors of judgment rather than deliberate disobedience. Once you have made the decision to walk as Jesus did, it will grieve you to grieve Him. When you make mistakes, or fail to take the necessary action because of human weakness, you can receive God's forgiveness. There is no condemnation for you because of that passing failure. Allow that failure to increase your desire for obedience in the future.

The fear of failure should not prevent you from making a firm decision to follow Jesus. You are simply agreeing to put the teaching of Jesus into practice, regardless of what others do or say. Some may accuse you of taking your discipleship too seriously, or will claim that it is impracticable to follow Jesus so closely in modern society. Stand firm against such suggestions and lovingly and graciously make it clear that you will not compromise your obedience to the Lord Jesus Christ.

BENEFITS OF OBEDIENCE

To set your heart on doing what Jesus would do will produce many positive benefits in your life. Obviously, some of your attitudes towards people, money, business practices and social responsibility are likely to change. Any changes will be for the better, if they bring your life into a closer conformity to the life of Jesus Himself.

God gives you both His Word and His Spirit to help you understand His will for you. You will become more sensitive to the voice of the Holy Spirit and more willing to respond to His leading. You will experience God's refining out of your life many negative thoughts, attitudes and actions, inconsistent with the life of Jesus.

When you desire to act like Him, He will give you the faith to do so. Faith and love will be the governing principles of your actions, words and attitudes. You will become more patient and tolerant of others, more willing to forgive them. You will have a greater compassion for those in need and a greater concern for the lost.

All these changes will be positive and will make you a more whole person. The more like Jesus you are, the healthier you will be in every way. You inherit everything from God that He inherits, if you are willing to share His suffering now so that you may also share in His glory. Even when obedience proves costly you will not be the loser, for God will always give back to you infinitely more than you have given to Him, both in this life and, eternally, in heaven.

Changes will take place in you because God wants to see

those changes. Many of the old habits will go! Submit willingly to these changes and resist the temptation to return to those old habits and so compromise your discipleship.

By taking your discipleship seriously you will be seeking first the Kingdom of God and His righteousness. You can be confident that God will keep His promise to you and meet your every need, as He did with Jesus.

You will pray with greater purpose and faith, for you will want to pray as Jesus would, meeting every situation with His faith, gaining His perspective on the various circumstances in which you are placed. Remember that Jesus promises to do anything you ask in His name.

When others challenge you as to why you make the decisions you make, do not deny your Lord or avoid the issue. State simply that you have decided to act as you believe Jesus would have acted in your position. Trust that God will use that as both a witness, an inspiration and a challenge to others.

You can make this simple covenant, or agreement, with the Lord, realising that this states in simple terms what it means to be a disciple, one who seeks to live as a child of the Kingdom of God:

I will ask myself the question: what would Jesus do?
I will then do what He would do in my position.
I will apply this question to all my actions.
I will do what Jesus would do regardless of the cost to myself.
I will ask for God's help by the Holy Spirit to enable me to walk as Jesus did.
I understand that I shall not be under any condemnation when I fail, but it is my honest intention to seek God's will in every situation. I want to be a true disciple and live as a child of the positive Kingdom.

It would be good to copy this agreement, sign it and keep it in your Bible. On the first day of every month you can reaffirm your decision to walk as Jesus did and pray for God's continued help to enable you to do so.

Chapter 18

THE HEAVENLY REWARD

To live Kingdom life *now* is to do what Jesus would do in your position, regardless of the cost. Your citizenship is already in heaven. But it is not enough to rejoice in your inheritance; God expects your life to be lived in a manner worthy of such an inheritance. He expects a life of faith and love as evidence that He is your life.

Paul tells the Thessalonians that they will be counted worthy of the Kingdom (for which they were then suffering persecution), because both their faith and their love of one another was increasing. (2 Thess. 1: 3–5) Obviously the Holy Spirit was watering the seed of the Kingdom in their lives, so that they were increasingly fruitful even in adverse circumstances. Paul prays that God may count them worthy of His calling, and by His power He may fulfil every good purpose of theirs and 'every act prompted by your faith.' (v 11) He wants to see Jesus glorified in them and for them to be glorified in Him, by the grace of God the Father and His Son.

To live a life of Kingdom faith will require perseverance. Jesus said: 'No-one who puts his hand to the plough and looks back is fit for service in the kingdom of God.' (Luke 9: 62) There will be constant pressure from the world, the flesh and the devil, to compromise your obedience to Him.

We can be adept at finding excuses for not putting Jesus first. When some tried to delay following Him, He retorted 'Let the dead bury their own dead, but you go and proclaim the kingdom of God.' (Luke 9: 60)

Christians are made holy, to be holy. They are to be like Jesus. That will never be accomplished by trying to imitate Him in their own strength, but only through His life being expressed through them. The seed of the Kingdom is planted within them so that, watered by the Spirit, that seed will grow to maturity. A life of submission to the authority of the King is evidence of this.

The eternal life, the fullness of God's life, given him in Jesus, will result in more of the Lord shining through the believer's life; more of Jesus will be seen in him.

Paul persevered until the end of his life in fulfilling the commission given him by God. Even when in detention in Rome: 'From morning till evening he explained and declared to them the kingdom of God.' (Acts 28: 23) For two whole years 'Boldly and without hindrance he preached the kingdom of God and taught about the Lord Jesus Christ.' (v. 31) The result was that even in Caesar's household there were those who had accepted the gospel and had received the inheritance of the Kingdom.

Jesus makes it clear to His disciples that to live the life of the Kingdom in an ungodly society will prove costly. Being part of the Kingdom does not mean they will be spared troubles and difficulties: 'In this world you will have trouble. But take heart! I have overcome the world.' (John 16: 33)

The children of the Kingdom can live in the victory of the King, even though they may suffer persecution and rejection. Tribulation, persecution and rejection are inevitable if God's children are to live in this negative world.

Jesus says: 'Blessed are those who are persecuted because of righteousness, for theirs is the kingdom of heaven. Blessed are you when people insult you, persecute you and falsely say all kinds of evil against you because of me. Rejoice and be glad, because great is your reward in heaven, for in the same way they persecuted the prophets who were before you.' (Matt. 5: 10–12)

Living the life of the positive Kingdom of light amid the

negative kingdom of darkness, is clearly not going to be easy. Jesus Himself did not have an easy time, experiencing much opposition especially from the religious traditionalists, who were more concerned about the outward performance of their rites and ceremonies than about spiritual rebirth.

To live a life of righteousness amid unrighteousness or self-righteousness, is inevitably going to produce conflicts. Because Satan's kingdom is one based on lies and deception, it is inevitable that those seeking to live in the truth and righteousness of Jesus, will be on the receiving end of slander and insult.

The people are reminded by Jesus that, no matter what opposition is encountered because of their faith in Him, those who are part of His Kingdom can afford to rejoice and be glad amid all their difficulties, for their heavenly reward is assured. Beyond their life and witness in this world, they will be able to enjoy all the privileges of the Kingdom without any such opposition.

INCREASING OPPOSITION

Jesus speaks, not only of the presence of the Kingdom, but also of its future manifestation, when the sovereignty of Jesus will be established everywhere as He returns in triumph.

Before that event the children of the Kingdom can expect to suffer an increase in opposition and persecution. There will be many false Christs, wars and rumours of wars, famines and earthquakes. But there will be no need for them to be alarmed. 'For I will give you words and wisdom that none of your adversaries will be able to resist or contradict.' (Luke 21: 15) Such things must happen and are the beginning of birth pain heralding the coming of the new order. 'When you see these things happening, you know that the kingdom of God is near.' (v. 31)

'Then you will be handed over to be persecuted and put to death, and you will be hated by all nations because of me. At that time many will turn away from the faith and will betray and hate each other'. (Matt. 24: 9–10) False prophets will deceive and there will be an increase in wickedness. Many people's love for God will grow cold in this time of severe testing, 'but he who stands firm to the end will be saved.' (v. 13)

Christians in some nations have been through times of testing, but it seems that Jesus is warning there will be greater trials ahead. These will demonstrate who truly are the children of the Kingdom. They will not fall away, because they will not deny the King who reigns over them.

It is natural to wonder if you would be able to endure such testing yourself. That is not a proper question. To the faithful God will always supply the grace to remain faithful. In a time of severe testing, you would have all the resources of the Kingdom available to you. Through faith in Jesus you could draw on these resources, knowing that He would not leave you, fail you or forsake you.

Jesus promises: 'And this gospel of the kingdom will be preached in the whole world as a testimony to all nations, and then the end will come.' (v. 14) There will be a world-wide proclamation of the truth, of God's offer of the Kingdom to those who acknowledge His sovereignty.

The Son of man will come 'on the clouds of the sky, with power and great glory. And he will send his angels with a loud trumpet call, and they will gather his elect from the four winds, from one end of the heavens to the other.' (vv. 30–1) The elect are the children of the Kingdom!

Jesus urges His disciples to 'keep watch, because you do not know on what day your Lord will come.' (Matt. 24: 42) They are to be prepared like the faithful and wise servant who was trusted to give his household food at the proper time while the master was away. Such a servant will be put 'in charge of all his possessions.' (Matt. 24: 47) He will enter into the full inheritance of the Kingdom he has experienced only partially, but has served faithfully.

By contrast, the wicked servant beats his fellow servants and eats and drinks with drunkards. The master of that servant will come when he least expects him. 'He will cut him to pieces and assign him a place with the hypocrites, where there will be weeping and gnashing of teeth.' (v. 51)

THE TEN VIRGINS

The alternatives seem clear! To emphasise the point Jesus gives the parable of the Ten Virgins. The Kingdom of heaven will be like ten virgins who took their lamps and went out to meet the bridegroom. Five were wise and five foolish. The foolish ones took their lamps, but no oil; the wise took flasks of oil as well as their lamps.

The bridegroom was a long time in coming and they all fell asleep. When they were awoken at midnight by shouts heralding his imminent arrival, the foolish asked the wise for some of their oil as their lamps were going out. The wise refused as they did not have enough for all. The foolish ones would have to go and buy fresh supplies of oil.

While they were gone, the bridegroom arrived. The wise virgins went with him into the banquet, and the door was shut. When the foolish returned and asked for the door to be opened, they were told by the bridegroom: 'I tell you the truth, I don't know you.' (Matt. 25: 12)

The lesson to learn is clear: 'Therefore keep watch, because you do not know the day or the hour.' (v. 13)

The bridegroom is Jesus, the wise virgins the faithful children of the Kingdom. In Scripture, oil is used to describe the Holy Spirit. It is by His Spirit that God, not only teaches what resources of the Kingdom are available to us; He also enables us to understand the signs of the times, to be prepared for the coming of Jesus. How important, therefore, that our lamps are full and we have oil to spare. If we are found wanting, there will be no point in turning to others for help, no time to acquire fresh oil. His fullness is always available to us and it is in that fullness that God intends us to live. 'And I pray that you, being rooted and established in love, may have power, together with all the saints, to grasp how wide and long and high and deep is the love of Christ, and to know this love that surpasses knowledge – that you may be filled to the measure of all the fullness of God.' (Eph. 3: 17–19)

FAITHFUL TO THE END

In the early chapters of Revelation God addresses letters to seven churches. In these He talks of overcoming the opposition and difficulties that each is confronted with, so they may receive their reward. The Spirit says: 'To him who overcomes, I will give the right to eat from the tree of life,' (Rev. 2: 7) meaning that we will enjoy eternal life in the final consummation of the Kingdom.

'Be faithful, even to the point of death, and I will give you the crown of life.' (v. 10) He who overcomes will not be hurt by the second death; he will not experience eternal death or separation from God.

Those who overcome will have authority over the nations; they will share the Messiah's kingly reign. They will receive hidden manna, be given entrance to the heavenly banquet. They will be dressed in white, the symbol of purity, and their names will never be erased from the book of life.

Each will be acknowledged by name before the Father and His angels. Jesus had promised: 'Whoever acknowledges me before men, I will also acknowledge him before my Father in heaven. But whoever disowns me before men, I will disown him before my Father in heaven.' (Matt. 10: 32–3)

He who overcomes will be a pillar in God's temple, another assurance of being part of the final, victorious manifestation of the Kingdom. 'Never again will he leave it.' He will even have the Lord's name written on him as a sign both of His possession and protection. And he will be given 'the right to sit with me on my throne, just as I overcame and sat down with my Father on his throne.' (Rev. 3: 21)

Such promises are immense in their implications, but do point to the need to be faithful; that as children of the Kingdom nothing will be allowed to hinder us from entering into our full inheritance.

The man who abides in Jesus has nothing to fear. He seeks first the Kingdom and is concerned to walk in holiness and righteousness with the Lord, loving, giving and serving faithfully. These are not to be seen as conditions to entering the Kingdom of heaven, but as the natural consequence of already being part of that Kingdom. There needs to be no fear of judgment for anyone who lives to please the Lord.

THE TALENTS

A man entrusted his property to his servants while away on a journey. To one he gave five talents of silver, to another two and to another one, 'each according to his ability.' (Matt. 25: 15) 'The man who had received the five talents went at once and put his money to work and gained five more. So also, the one with the two talents gained two more. But the man who had received the one talent went off, dug a hole in the ground and hid his master's money.' (vv. 16–18)

It was a long time before the master returned and settled accounts with them. The first said: 'Master, you entrusted me with five talents. See, I have gained five more.' (v. 20) His master was delighted: 'Well done, good and faithful servant! You have been faithful with a few things; I will put you in charge of many things. Come and share your master's happiness!' (v. 21)

The man with the two talents had gained two more and received the same commendation from his master. The third said: 'Master, I knew that you are a hard man, harvesting where you have not sown and gathering where you have not scattered seed. So I was afraid and went out and hid your talent in the ground. See, here is what belongs to you.' (vv. 24–5)

The master was furious with him. He should at least have

deposited the money with bankers to gain interest on it. 'Take the talent from him,' he commanded, 'and give it to the one who has the ten talents. For everyone who has will be given more, and he will have an abundance. Whoever does not have, even what he has will be taken from him. And throw that worthless servant outside, into the darkness, where there will be weeping and gnashing of teeth.' (vv. 28–30)

If God entrusts us with His riches, spiritual and material, He expects them to be used faithfully and fruitfully. If He has planted the seed of His Kingdom in our lives, He expects us to produce Kingdom fruit.

In the parable of the Sower, the seed planted in good soil could produce good fruit, but in varying quantities. Jesus makes a similar point in the parable of the Talents: different people have different capacities. God does not expect a man to produce fruit beyond his capacity; but He does desire that each bears fruit to the full extent of his capacity.

The fruit is the reproduction of the seed or of the talents. The seed sown is the seed of the Kingdom. The talents represent the gifts and rich resources God makes available to the children of His Kingdom.

The master is delighted with those who are fruitful according to their respective abilities, and they are promised great responsibility and a share in his joy – a promise of inheritance in the Kingdom of heaven, where they will be able to know God's joy eternally.

The third servant suffers a different fate. Once again we are faced with evidence of God's wrath that will be vented in judgment on the disobedient. The servant had received from the master, but wasted his inheritance; he was unfruitful, he was unfaithful. The judgment: he would lose what he had.

Again Jesus reiterates an important spiritual principle; 'For everyone who has will be given more, and he will have an abundance.' When we are fruitful, seeking first God's Kingdom and righteousness, He lavishes His provision on us. We want for nothing. He demonstrates His love and care for us. When we give to Him in any way, He always gives more back to us; He always outdoes us in giving.

When we are unfruitful or hold back from giving, we thereby impoverish ourselves. It is not that God wants to withhold His blessings and abundance from us; we are not fulfilling the spiritual principles of the Kingdom that Jesus taught. The more of His resources we put to fruitful use, the more He gives.

On the other hand: 'Whoever does not have, even what he has will be taken from him.' The man who is unfruitful will lose even what he appears to have. We must not side-step the things that Jesus said because we do not like them, or because they do not fit in with concepts of the kind of Lord we want Him to be. There is no point in trying to spiritualise the message of this parable out of existence. What Jesus says is simple: the man with one talent proved unfruitful, the talent was taken from him, he was judged as worthless and ordered to be cast into outer darkness.

This is in full accord with what Jesus teaches elsewhere. When describing Himself as the True Vine, He described the disciples as branches. No branch can bear fruit by itself; it must remain in the vine. The man who does so will bear much fruit. He does not have to produce the fruit himself or be anxious about the level of fruitfulness in his life. By abiding in Jesus he will be fruitful. The sap of the Holy Spirit will flow through his 'branch' and produce the fruit.

The Father will prune the fruitful branches to make them more fruitful still. But Jesus also says; 'He cuts off every branch in me that bears no fruit'. (John 15: 2) What happens to such branches? 'If anyone does not remain in me, he is like a branch that is thrown away and withers; such branches are picked up, thrown into the fire and burned.' (v. 6)

Jesus is not afraid of warning people of the eternal consequences of rejecting Him, of their unbelief or unfruitfulness.

Does this mean that those who have received the gift of the

Kingdom from God should fear losing their inheritance? Not at all. The Father does expect them to remain faithful to the end; and he will keep them faithful, if their hearts are set upon pleasing Him. 'May God himself, the God of peace, sanctify you through and through. May your whole spirit, soul and body be kept blameless at the coming of our Lord Jesus Christ. The one who calls you is faithful and he will do it.' (1 Thess. 5: 23–4)

BEFORE THE THRONE

After the parable of the talents, Jesus talks of His second coming; 'When the Son of Man comes in his glory, and all the angels with him, he will sit on his throne in heavenly glory. All the nations will be gathered before him, and he will separate the people one from another as a shepherd separates the sheep from the goats. He will put the sheep on his right and the goats on his left.' (Matt. 25: 31–3) This is consistent with what Jesus taught when explaining the parable of the Weeds.

The King will say to those on the right, 'Come, you who are blessed by my Father; take your inheritance, the kingdom prepared for you since the creation of the world.' (v. 34) They are invited to be part of the great consummation of the Kingdom because they have proved faithful and fruitful. By their correctness of liturgical practice or doctrine; by their strict observance and loyalty to tradition? No! By the practical outworking of Kingdom principles in their lives, reaching out into the world with the love and resources of the King. 'For I was hungry and you gave me something to eat, I was thirsty and you gave me something to drink, I was a stranger and you invited me in, I needed clothes and you clothed me, I was sick and you looked after me, I was in prison and you came to visit me.' (Matt. 25: 35–6)

The righteous ones, the sheep, the Kingdom people, are amazed at this assessment of their lives and ask when they did such things for the Lord; to which the King replies: 'I tell you the truth, whatever you did for one of the least of these brothers of mine, you did for me.' (v. 40)

Why their perplexity? Because their hearts were full of the love God had given them it seemed only natural and right to do such things, as the opportunities were presented to them. They responded quietly to God's call to express His love in these ways, without any thought of reward. They did them because they loved the Lord and desired to walk in right ways with Him. Because they loved Him, they loved people and welcomed the opportunities to love and serve in His name.

The goats are given a very different judgment: 'Depart from me, you who are cursed, into the eternal fire prepared for the devil and his angels.' (v. 41) They had received similar opportunities to love and serve, but had not responded to them. They too are taken aback by the judgment, but for different reasons. There is a sense of bewilderment, of resentment and indignation in their reply: 'Lord, when did we see you hungry or thirsty or a stranger or needing clothes or sick or in prison, and did not help you?' (v. 44) The implication is that if they knew it had been the Lord Himself they would have given to Him; but it was only people!

The King replies to them: 'I tell you the truth, whatever you did not do for one of the least of these, you did not do for me.' (v. 45) And Jesus sums up by saying: 'Then they will go away to eternal punishment, but the righteous to eternal life.' (v. 46)

This shows how intensely practical Kingdom living is, bringing love and service to those in need, expressing the compassion and mercy of God. How easy to have the wrong motives, expecting to be thanked, praised, recognised, admired even!

Kingdom children quietly get on with the job, not for any appreciation or reward, but simply out of love. They not only have a position of righteousness before God because of all that Jesus has done for them; they seek to live in righteousness, doing in each situation what He wants them to do, what He would have done Himself in the days of His humanity.

What a warning for the super-spiritual, those who are full of the right-sounding religious jargon, but who fail to produce the fruit of the Spirit in their lives! What a warning for those who do not want the quiet comfort of their lives invaded by the needs of others!

Jesus had said to the religious leaders: 'Woe to you, teachers of the law and Pharisees, you hypocrites! You give a tenth of your spices – mint, dill and cummin. But you have neglected the more important matters of the law – justice, mercy and faithfulness.' (Matt. 23: 23)

Who, then, are the righteous? Those who have come to Jesus in repentance and faith. They are washed in His blood and made righteous in God's sight. They are the children of His Kingdom by His grace and mercy. They have new hearts and have been given new life. The Holy Spirit lives in them and bears fruit in their lives. Because they have submitted to the sovereignty and authority of Jesus, they want His will above their own, to express His love and compassion to those in need, loving their brethren as He has loved them, and reaching out into the world with the truth and power of the positive Kingdom.

And who are the goats? Those who have rejected the King and demonstrate that rejection by the way in which they treat His brethren. That does not mean they are devoid of good works. But no amount of good works can justify a person in God's sight!

Jesus is pointing out that true righteousness, borne out of a true experience of new birth, will be expressed in practical ways. Faith will produce good works; but good works will not produce faith – and without faith it is impossible to please God.

The righteous need not fear judgment. The unrighteous, on the other hand, face the eternal punishment of which Jesus warns. Christians cannot afford to be complacent. The believer, who has assurance in his heart of his salvation, is full of zeal to share his faith with others, to see the lost drawn into the Kingdom, to express his love for Jesus in practical ways by loving others.

Chapter 19

KINGDOM GLORY

There is glory to come for all the children of the Kingdom, for their King will return to the earth in triumph. They are to prepare for that time, not knowing when it will be, but living as if it is to be today.

Whenever there has been revival in the Church's history, there has been expectancy of Christ's return, accompanied by a sense of urgency in the preaching of the Kingdom. His return will be a glorious event for the saved, but will involve judgment for the lost. Renewed faith in the great hope that God's Kingdom will be established and recognised everywhere, brings with it the sense of urgency in reaching as many of the lost as possible with the truth, so that they may have opportunity to repent of their sins and be born again into the Kingdom of God.

'In the presence of God and of Christ Jesus, who will judge the living and the dead, and in view of his appearing and his kingdom, I give you this charge: Preach the Word; be prepared in season and out of season; correct, rebuke and encourage – with great patience and careful instruction.' (2 Tim. 4: 1–2)

Jesus did not wait until His disciples were theologically trained before sending them out with the good news of the Kingdom. They had a divine commission; they were being sent out in the name of the King of heaven. If people received them, well and good; if not, they had clear instructions: 'But when you enter a town and are not welcomed, go into its streets and say, "Even the dust of your town that sticks to our feet we wipe off against you. Yet be sure of this: The kingdom of God is near." ' (Luke 10: 10–11)

REVIVAL

We live in exciting times. A spiritual revival has begun in some parts of the world, and with it the expectation that the Second Coming of the King is imminent. There is an increasing sense of urgency in reaching the lost with the gospel, a realisation that there can be no answer to the dilemmas of modern society, except a spiritual one. Jesus Christ is the only answer to men's needs, individually and socially. He is the Way, and the gospel of the Kingdom the means, by which a spiritual revolution is to take place in the coming generation.

We can only marvel at being chosen by God, not only to be alive at such a time as this, but to be included in His divine purpose. We can rejoice that our names are written in heaven and that we are sent out to heal the sick, spiritually, emotionally, physically and socially; to declare that 'The Kingdom of God is near.' We have the divine commission and He is ready to anoint all who will go in obedience to His command.

It is encouraging to see many young people, especially men, being called to full-time ministry. Some are being called to ordination in the historic denominations, but by no means all. The variety of New Testament ministries are being restored to the Church. God is firing the hearts of many with a new enthusiasm and zeal for the Kingdom, and is equipping them with the power of His Spirit for His service. It seems God is raising up an army, and is appointing officers to be trained to lead a great march against the powers of darkness that reign rampant over many places, holding the lives of multitudes in spiritual, moral and even physical bondage.

This is not wishful thinking, it is happening; and the

spiritually discerning see that it is happening. God is calling for faith among His children, for they are to proclaim not a Kingdom of words but of power. With the verbal proclamation there is to be evidence of signs and wonders. What we have seen in recent years, great as that has been, is only the prelude to the greater things we are about to see.

The Lord is not only asking His people to pray for revival, but to be themselves revived. Out of that will come the urgent desire to reach the lost, to be faithful witnesses; and still more will hear God's call to lay aside all other considerations of personal gain and ambition, to be available totally to the King.

WITNESSES

Others will sense the importance of their Kingdom witness in their prevailing circumstances at work, with neighbours, friends and especially among their own families.

God is wanting not only faith, but an increase of love among His children. The closer they draw near to Him who is love, the more they will sense His love for them; the more they will know love for Him and for others, and the more willing they will be to live Kingdom life. For they will acknowledge how their love of sin has not only deprived them of enjoying many of the Kingdom riches God has made available to them, but has also had a negative effect on their witness to others. It is difficult for the world to believe that the Kingdom is at hand, if it is difficult to see evidence of the Kingdom among Christians.

'Love the Lord your God with all your heart and with all your soul and with all your strength and with all your mind', (Luke 10: 27) and your neighbour as yourself, is still God's purpose.

God is calling His children back to holiness, to be like Jesus, to be people full of His Spirit, men and woman of faith and love; those who recognise that God has set them apart for

Himself. He has separated them from sin so that they can live in righteousness, living lives pleasing to Him.

God is confronting His children with the areas of compromise in their lives. He is showing them that they cannot please both God and men. In pleasing God they will be able to minister more effectively to men. It is a time, not to be conformed to the pattern of this world, but to be transformed by having our minds renewed, by having them set on things above, on pleasing the King and living as Kingdom children.

REAPING

It is a time of reaping. The fields are white and ready for harvest. It is God's moment when we will see the greatest harvest of souls the world has ever seen, as the gospel of the Kingdom is faithfully lived and proclaimed. This is true already in several nations in different parts of the world; it will be more widely the case in the coming years.

This does not mean that the way ahead will be easy. Wherever there is a major thrust forward of the gospel, the forces of darkness gather to oppose the spread of the Kingdom. Those who exercise their Kingdom faith and authority are not daunted by opposition, because they know already the outcome of the conflict.

It is God's time to possess the land, to see a return to faith in God's Word and the demonstrations of His power; to see His love shed abroad in the way lives are manifestly transformed. Instead of selfishness and waste, there will be selfless giving to others. Instead of pride, men and women will humble themselves under the mighty hand of God.

It is a time for righteousness to be restored:

If your hand causes you to sin, cut it off. It is better for you to enter life maimed than with two hands to go into hell, where the fire never goes out. And if your foot causes you to sin, cut it off. It is better for you to enter life crippled than to have two feet and be thrown into hell. And if your eye causes you to sin, pluck it out. It is better for you to enter the kingdom of God with one eye than to have two eyes and be thrown into hell. (Mark 9: 43–7).

God's timing for revival is linked with His children's willingness to seek Him, with their desire to be godly and to be used by Him in prayer and action to reach the lost. Revival is costly. Those that have wanted nothing to do with the renewal we have seen in recent years, certainly will not want to face the cost of revival.

And yet when hearts are set aflame with love for God, the cost does not seem important. It is never too costly to please the one you truly love. When we want to satisfy ourselves in some way, we leave nothing undone that could contribute to the success of our aims. When we want to please the King, we will not count obedience too costly; we will be more aware of the honour accorded us from heaven.

It was so out of place for the mother of James and John to ask Jesus that they might sit on either side of Him in His Kingdom. (Matt. 20: 21) We do not serve Him for any honour to be accorded to us either on earth or in heaven. Neither are we obedient to His commands to gain entrance into His Kingdom. We serve, love and obey because we have been given such a wonderful inheritance and want others to share in the joy of the Lord. 'Blessed is the man who will eat at the feast in the kingdom of God.' (Luke 14: 15)

To His disciples Jesus said: 'And I confer on you a kingdom, just as my Father conferred one on me, so that you may eat and drink at my table in my kingdom and sit on thrones, judging the twelve tribes of Israel.' (Luke 22: 29–30) Not all of us will judge in that way, but all who are faithful to the King are invited to the marriage supper of the Lamb of God. 'Here I am! I stand at the door and knock. If anyone hears my voice and opens the door, I will come in and eat with him, and he with me.' (Rev. 3: 20)

HIS MAJESTY REVEALED

When the Lord announces His return to John, He says: 'Behold, I am coming soon! My reward is with me, and I will give to everyone according to what he has done.' (Rev. 22: 12) Those who have availed themselves of His redeeming love will enjoy that heavenly reward: 'Blessed are those who wash their robes, that they may have the right to the tree of life and may go through the gates into the city. Outside are the dogs, those who practise magic arts, the sexually immoral, the murderers, the idolaters and everyone who loves and practises falsehood.' (Rev. 22: 14–15)

Throughout Scripture there is the contrast between the faithful who humble themselves before God, and the proud who set themselves up against Him by the flagrant disobedience in their lives.

Not only will the Kingdom children feast at the heavenly banquet; they will reign on the earth; 'with your blood you purchased men for God from every tribe and language and people and nation. You have made them to be a kingdom and priests to serve our God, and they will reign on the earth.' (Rev. 5: 9–10)

The provisional manner in which the Kingdom can be manifested now, its secret hidden from many, will give way to the open manifestation of the majesty of Jesus when all will be revealed. Satan and his demons will be condemned to their eternal torment. They have tormented men for centuries and will receive their just reward for their rebellion against God.

Satan will be cast down and the saints of God, the children of the Kingdom, will receive their full inheritance. 'The kingdom of the world has become the kingdom of our Lord and of his Christ, and he will reign for ever and ever.' (Rev. 11: 15)

The elders who surround the throne worship the Lord

because He has taken His great power and has begun to reign universally. This is the time for judgment and for rewarding 'your saints and those who reverence your name, both small and great – and for destroying those who destroy the earth.' (Rev. 11: 18)

Satan's defeat is final. No longer will he be able to accuse the brethren: 'Now have come the salvation and the power and the kingdom of our God, and the authority of his Christ. For the accuser of our brothers, who accuses them before our God day and night, has been hurled down. They overcame him by the blood of the Lamb and by the word of their testimony'. (Rev. 12: 10–11)

Jesus saw His own death as a release into the glory of the Kingdom from which He had come. The whole passion narrative is pregnant with the significance of what is happening in relation to the Kingdom. As Jesus is greeted with cries of 'Hosanna' on His triumphal entry into Jerusalem, some of the crowd shout: 'Blessed is the coming kingdom of our father David!' (Mark 11: 10)

When He blesses the cup at the Last Supper, He says: 'I tell you the truth, I will not drink again of the fruit of the vine until that day when I drink it anew in the kingdom of God.' (Mark 14: 25) He tells the disciples that He will not eat the Passover again until 'it finds fulfilment in the kingdom of God.' (Luke 22: 16) He will not drink of the fruit of the vine 'until the kingdom of God comes.' (v. 18)

The penitent thief crucified alongside Jesus asks Him to 'remember me when you come into your kingdom.' (Luke 23: 42) For the Christian, death is not a defeat but release in the full manifestation of God's glory.

The Christian has both entered the Kingdom and awaits its coming. Meanwhile he lives to praise and exalt the King. Psalm 145 is a great hymn exalting the majesty of God and the glory of His Kingdom.

Each generation will be able to tell of His mighty acts and 'speak of the glorious splendour of your majesty'. (v. 5) The saints, those redeemed by Jesus, 'will tell of the glory of your kingdom and speak of your might, so that all men may know of your mighty acts and the glorious splendour of your kingdom.' (vv. 11–12)

These are prophecies that relate to this, as to every other, generation. It is we who are to extol the promises of our heavenly King and tell men of the glory of His Kingdom, because we have experience of that ourselves. We cannot speak of what we do not know. If we know the Kingdom as a reality, we know not only of its future hope, but of its present power. We can tell, therefore, of the mighty acts our God performs in demonstration of His Kingly presence among men.

And yet the greater revelation of His glory awaits us. 'Your kingdom is an everlasting kingdom, and your dominion endures through all generations.' (v. 13)

Jesus says that a kingdom divided against itself will fall. Satan's dominion is divided and his ultimate demise together with all who gain their authority from him, is assured.

Those who honour King Jesus will in turn be honoured by Him. Meanwhile we have the opportunity and the responsibility to declare to this generation by word and power the glorious good news of the gospel of the Kingdom. Our faith needs to rise to embrace the purposes of God that, before the great and final conflict, many will embrace the King as they respond to His offer to give them the Kingdom.

And may He continue to remove from our hearts and lives every negative thought, desire, motive and intention that hinders the growth of Kingdom life within us. As He takes out the negative, may He continue to pour into our hearts and lives all the positive power of His Holy Spirit to enable us to live in Kingdom faith, expressing Kingdom love and exercising Kingdom power and authority.

'Thank you, heavenly Father, for your positive Kingdom.'

Colin Urquhart

HOLY FIRE

'The Holy Fire of God's Spirit needs to work with purifying, refining power among His own people. The Holy Fire needs to inflame the hearts of His children with renewed love and zeal for His ways.'

Many today are praying for a spiritual awakening in their nation. But revival, writes Colin Urquhart, has to begin among Christians.

Drawing on his own experience of God's Spirit, and basing his teaching firmly on Scripture, Colin Urquhart shows how Christians can lead holy lives. 'It is to holiness of life that every child of God is called.'

Colin Urquhart

FAITH FOR THE FUTURE

After five richly-blessed years at St Hugh's, Luton, Colin Urquhart felt that God was calling him to a new ministry – to be 'heard among the nations.' His step of faith into the unknown was the start of a miraculous adventure, told in this inspiring sequel to **When The Spirit Comes.**

Colin's international ministry of renewal, healing and evangelism is now touching and transforming lives all over the world.